orgasmic
APPETIZERS
AND MATCHING WINES

Tiny Bites with the MOAN FACTOR

Shari Darling

Whitecap Books

Whitecap Books is known for its expertise in the cookbook market, and has produced some of the most innovative and familiar titles found in kitchens across North America.

Edited by Kate Zimmerman
Proofread by Lesley Cameron
Design by Sun Ngo
Cover design by Michelle Mayne
Photographs by Steve Livingston
Food styling by Shari Darling

Other photographs courtesy of:
Wine Institute of California, Australian Wine Export Council, Niko Coutroulis, Argentina Winery, Altavista (Argentina Wine Company), Premium Port Wines, Dairy Farmers of Canada

Illustrations on pages 8, 19 and 39 are courtesy of the Umami Information Center. Visit their website at www.umamiinfo.com or contact them at:
5th Floor, MS Building
17-6 Ichiban-cho, Chiyoda-ku
Tokyo, Japan 102-0082
or
c/o Cross Media Inc.
66 Wells Street
London, UK W1T 3PY

Printed in China

Library and Archives Canada Cataloguing in Publication

Darling, Shari
   Orgasmic appetizers and matching wines : tiny bites with the moan factor / Shari Darling.

Includes index.
ISBN 978-1-55285-923-0 (pbk.)

   1. Appetizers. 2. Wine and wine making.
I. Title.

TX740.D38 2008   641.812   C2008-902142-8

The publisher acknowledges the financial support of the Government of Canada through the Book Publishing Industry Development Program (BPIDP) and the Province of British Columbia through the Book Publishing Tax Credit.

08 09 10 11 12 5 4 3 2 1

Judith
Here's to the
molecular
Chemo!
Shane O'Farrell

> **"When we try out a new dish,
> one that does not belong to the family
> culinary repertoire, we have the same
> feeling Christopher Columbus had
> setting out to discover the New World."**

HERVÉ THIS, *MOLECULAR GASTRONOMY*

table of contents

*P*reface

I love hosting dinner parties. Over the years, I've noticed that each meal has elicited from my guests different levels of culinary appreciation. Sometimes they've simply thanked me while heading out the door at the end of the evening. Other times, guests have generously shared the discoveries they've made and insights they've had during the meal and have expressed their appreciation for my ability to harmonize wines with simple dishes.

I recently discovered an entirely new level of culinary appreciation. One evening, I was hired to host an exclusive wine tasting for a group of local businesswomen who were also longtime friends. I prepared various appetizers with matching wines to be enjoyed before the actual wine tasting. Wild Mushroom & Brie Bruschetta was one of the appetizers (see page 173). I served an Australian Shiraz, as its tastes and flavors worked particularly well with the simple ingredients and seasonings in the bruschetta.

As the women began to nibble on the bruschetta and sip the wine, I noticed that they had stopped talking. Instead, they were chiming in together on what sounded like a version of the Eastern mantra, "Om." When I looked at a few of their faces, however, I realized that the women were not chanting, but rather moaning in delight.

At that moment I realized that beyond the possibility of creating harmony on the palate through a wine and food partnership—as

explained in my cookbook, *Harmony on the Palate*—there is an even higher realm of culinary pleasure. It is that ecstatic moment, when a food and wine pairing reveals itself as completely magical, that I describe as the MOAN FACTOR.

Moaning is an involuntary release, an expulsion of air and sound. When a wine and food partnership tastes sublime, our senses— sight, sound, touch, smell and taste (as they pertain to taste, flavor and texture)—are heightened. It's an experience that allows us to get much more out of eating than mere survival. It's spiritual. It's spine-tingling. It's ecstatic. I call it a "culinary orgasm."

THE PURPOSE OF THIS COOKBOOK

The culinary orgasm is sometimes just a happy accident. As a home cook (I'm not a chef), I love to hear my guests moaning over my food and wine choices. I also love to hear my romantic partner—my husband, Jack—do the same. For many of us, provoking this sublime response in others is hit and miss. What if you could learn the science and art of causing the culinary orgasm by purposefully preparing hedonistic recipes and matching wines, and you could produce them on a consistent and frequent basis? Who wouldn't want to master the MOAN FACTOR?

In this book I share my research into the sources of the culinary orgasm and the results of my successful experiments in achieving the most sensuous pairings. I share my ideas with you in hopes that you'll use them to cause a few orgasms for yourself, your sweetheart and your guests.

WHY APPETIZERS?

Appetizers are indulgent and irresistible, risky and exciting. They're sexy! They're meant to whet your appetite before the main meal. Appetizers please our eyes, ears, nose, palate and even our hands. As bite-sized morsels, appetizers are also less risky for the conservative eater. Even apprehensive types will often try at least one. These finger foods serve as a delightful way to introduce international tastes and flavors to your guests and/or romantic partner. They also tell your dinner guests you care enough about them to take a little extra trouble.

Appetizers can be served at cocktail and office parties, wedding receptions, anniversary events, holiday celebrations and more. They're usually served on a communal platter, creating an ambience of sophistication, as well as feelings of sharing and therefore oneness among guests.

Appetizers can also be the centerpieces of intimate occasions. On Valentine's Day, how about starting the evening with Oyster Shooters, the experience completed by a chilled glass of Sauvignon Blanc? How about Tea–Infused Dark Chocolate Truffles paired with a glass of Cabernet Sauvignon just before a long, slow massage? Oysters and dark chocolate are aphrodisiacs. So is wine! The culinary combinations in this book are sure to get your taste buds tingling and your goose bumps popping.

Well-made appetizers can set the context, style, theme and mood of your occasion. Whether you're serving them to a group of people, or privately to your sweetheart, they allow you to experiment with a variety of tastes and flavors at one event and on a small scale.

Appetizers can also be addictive. Have you ever noticed a room full of people suddenly move like a swarm of bees toward a particular server holding a tray of appetizers? Have you ever had to muster self-control to refrain from licking your fingers while at a party? I have. Or have you found yourself eating far too many servings of the same appetizer because it's so delicious? Me too.

These favorites are the orgasmic appetizers, the ones of which we never tire, the ones with the MOAN FACTOR. This book tells you how to make them and how to make each one shine by serving it alongside its ideal mate, a delicious glass of wine.

Shari Darling

*I*ntroduction

When we break down one moment of dining pleasure to get to the heart of the culinary orgasm, we find many internal and external elements working together simultaneously to conjure up magic in a wine and food partnership. Part One of *Orgasmic Appetizers* deconstructs this magic from a simple, basic point of view. I aim to show you how to consciously and effortlessly reconstruct a culinary orgasm for yourself and others whenever you choose.

If you've read my last cookbook, *Harmony on the Palate*, then you will undoubtedly have an understanding of the elements within the first two sections. I suggest you read these sections anyway as they will help enforce your understanding of taste, flavor and texture, as well as the Building Block Principles.

In Part One you'll discover the following:

- The ways in which we sense taste, flavor and texture and how they play major roles in our enjoyment of wine with food

- Three Building Block Principles that will help you pair wine with food effectively

- How all our senses create this moment of bliss, the culinary orgasm

- The kind of taster you are and how that plays an important role in the amount of each ingredient you use while cooking, as well as the recipes that will cause you and your guests to experience a culinary orgasm

- How to combine specific ingredients and match them with certain wines to produce the MOAN FACTOR

- How to organize and enhance your next intimate affair or entertaining event

Just as our imaginations are infinite, so, too, are the possibilities of ingredient combinations and wine partnerships to create appetizers and wines with the MOAN FACTOR. This cookbook explores only some of your countless options. I encourage you to transform your kitchen into a science lab.

Part Two is made up of recipes and matching wine notes that my friends, family, Fleming College wine certificate students and I agree are orgasmic. Remember that, ultimately, the kind of taster you are will determine what is orgasmic to you. That's why it's important that you discover and use your own five senses in recreating these wine and food partnerships.

If you're a "nontaster" like me, you may want to increase the amounts of garlic and seasonings you add to each recipe. If you're a "super-taster," you may want to cut back on these ingredients. You'll learn about the kind of taster you are shortly.

The recipes that made the grade were those that not only thrilled my friends, relatives, students and me, but also had the same effect on my recipe testers.

USING A UNIFIED LANGUAGE

Throughout this book, I use food terms to describe both food and wine sensations. The reason is that wine terms are technical and, for most of us, do not provide any insight into how various taste and flavor sensations are experienced on our palates. Using culinary terms with which you're already familiar will also help you to understand how the taste and flavor sensations of both the food and the wine work together to create balance and harmony. Here are some examples of the food terms I use to describe both wine and food.

food term	technical terms
sourness	acidity
sweetness	residual sugar
bitterness	tannin
dryness	astringency
creamy	malolactic fermentation
fatty	viscosity
savory	umami
mouthfeel/ texture irritation	chemosensory
taste sensations balanced or imbalanced in wine	structure in wine
layers of flavors in wine	complexity in wine

"Chefs don't create from recipes. They create from tastes. They create in the same way that a composer 'hears' notes in the concert hall of the mind before anyone plays them on the keyboard. Kitchen artists draw on the knowledge acquired through years of study, long practice and a generous dollop of intuition…"

Gray Kunz and Peter Kaminsky,
The Elements of Taste

THE RECIPES

All the recipes—ingredients, herbs, spices and amounts—have been reworked to be wine savvy and to fall within my Building Block Principles for pairing success.

The recipes use ingredients that can be found in most local supermarkets. The key is to hunt for fresh, pure, local, ripe and quality items.

All the recipes were developed to serve four to six guests. If entertaining for more than six, double the recipe, if necessary. If you intend on using appetizers from this book for a more intimate affair, cut the recipe in half. You can also make the recipe as per the instructions and save a few leftovers for the following day. When I was testing the recipes, my husband, Jack, often consumed the entire platter of appetizers meant for four to six people. That was one indication that the appetizer made the grade— they were addictive and therefore orgasmic!

Each section celebrates ingredient combinations and recipes from around the world, but all the recipes within one section work with a specific style of wine.

The kind of taster you are will determine the amount of seasonings, herbs and spices you will want to incorporate into an appetizer to appeal to your own sense of taste. (See What Kind of Taster Are You? on page 16.) You may be the kind of cook who likes to follow recipe directions so faithfully that you become annoyed if the writer doesn't give you specific instructions as to whether the half teaspoon of finely chopped basil is flat or heaped. I encourage you to use this cookbook as a starting point. If you want guidance in terms of seasoning your appetizers, look to your own senses—sight, smell, taste, flavor and texture—and even your sense of sound. Yes, sound. The sound of a crunchy canapé can be enough to cause your stomach to growl. Look to your own taste profile and imagination when recreating these recipes. The idea is to use this cookbook as a foundation on which to build your own appetizer and wine matches so you can create your own culinary orgasms.

Wine Styles

Almost every wine region around the world produces an array of wine styles. One grape variety, such as Chardonnay, can be fermented in a whole range of styles, in one winery, one region and in wine regions around the world. That's why pairing your dish to a specific wine style is far more fun and effective than matching it to a certain grape variety. An appetizer highlighting triple cream brie works far better with a big, fat, buttery Chardonnay than it does with a delicate, unoaked one.

Choosing wine by its style, rather than its grape variety or region, makes the wine selection process quick and simple. This method also allows you to explore the world, finding wines that fall into your own taste preferences. Most of all, choosing wine by style allows you to find the right wine for every culinary experience. This cookbook aims to make the task of pairing appetizers to wine styles easy for you.

Part Two is divided into sections celebrating a variety of styles. This cookbook does not include all the wine styles produced around the world. For example, I don't discuss sherry, Madeira or other fortified wines here. I choose wine styles that my "wino" and foodie friends and I tend to drink on a daily basis.

The wine styles I cover are:

- Sparkling
- Crisp, dry white
- Well-balanced, medium-bodied, smooth white
- Big, fat white
- Off-dry white
- Dry and off-dry rosé

- Light, fruity red
- Red with forward fruit
- Austere red
- Late harvest and icewine
- Port and port-style wine

At the beginning of each section, you'll find a list of international wines that fall into each particular style. This way you can find wines that are best suited to your taste preferences and, at the same time, explore the wine regions of the world.

RECIPE WINE NOTES

Each recipe also includes a matching, two-part wine note. The first part is called "Building Blocks." This segment explains the scientific basis on which you'll learn to build a tangible and harmonious partnership between the suggested wine and its accompanying recipe. This part deals with the basic taste of a wine and its harmonizing ingredients (sourness, sweetness, saltiness, bitterness) and a few highly recognizable flavors (like fat and hot and spiciness) and how they work together or counteract each other to create an orgasmic partnership. (Read the first chapter, The Sense of Taste.)

The second part of the wine note is called "Flavors." It focuses on the art of wine and food pairing—the creation of your flavor design. I've provided my own, but I encourage you to explore your own sense of flavor. Our sense of flavor is as individualistic as our love of movies and books.

My hope is that you enjoy experimenting with these recipes and wine notes as much as I enjoyed developing them. As I said in my last cookbook, *Harmony on the Palate*, creating harmony between a wine and a dish makes your dining experience a perfect example of living in the moment. But causing your guests or sweetheart to experience a culinary orgasm is even more tantalizing. It's downright naughty.

It's time to explore . . .

1

the *science & art* of the *moan factor*

the Sense of taste

Biting into a luscious, juicy strawberry covered in a thin coating of bittersweet dark chocolate is utterly divine. This tiny treat allows us to experience and enjoy our simultaneous sensations of taste, flavor and mouthfeel. We relish the sweet and sour taste of the ripe strawberry. The chocolatey flavor is satisfying, its aromas releasing as we chew and wafting up through our olfactory canal. Last, our palate dances with the contrast of textures between this dense, soft and juicy fruit and its thin, crisp, chocolate coating.

A glass of wine is just as pleasurable to our senses. It possesses taste sensations (among them sour, sweet and bitter) and flavor sensations (like fatty, floral and smoky). And let's not forget wine's tantalizing textures, ranging from sharp and effervescent to heavy and creamy. These three sensations—taste, flavor and mouthfeel—are the source of our love of wine and food.

It's important to understand the potential effect of these simultaneous sensations so you can pair wine with food effectively. Serve an ounce of tawny port with a chocolate-dipped strawberry and experience a culinary orgasm. Pair this same treat with a brut (dry) sparkling wine and you'll experience an offensive, metallic taste. A wine can make or break your dining experience.

Understanding these sensations will allow you to purposefully and effectively create appetizer and wine combinations that aren't just harmonizing and tasty, but are heightened to possess the MOAN FACTOR.

The simultaneous sensations are:

- the basic taste sensations (sour, sweet, salty and bitter), experienced on the tongue
- the secondary taste sensations (spicy, metallic and astringent), generally experienced as aftertastes
- the flavor sensations that include our sense of smell, experienced through the nose (orthonasal olfaction) and through the inside of the mouth (retro-nasal olfaction)
- the sense of texture, or mouthfeel

Aromas and textures are covered in the next chapter. Let's look at basic and secondary tastes first.

BASIC TASTE SENSATIONS

Our basic taste sensations are considered survival mechanisms. We humans develop them while still in the womb. At birth, we have a well-developed sense of taste and can identify four basic and well-known sensations of sweet, sour, salty and bitter.

There is also a fifth taste sensation called "umami," responsible for the amplitude and continuity or persistence of deliciousness of wine and food. (See the chapter Who's Your Umami?) We also have the ability to discern secondary tastes: those that are metallic, hot and spicy and astringent.

A map of taste

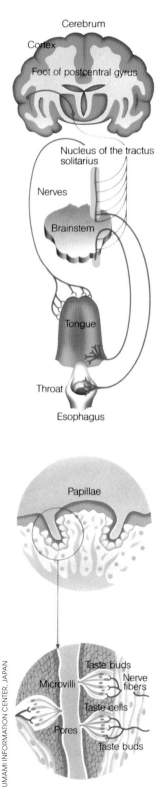

Cerebrum

Cortex

Foot of postcentral gyrus

Nucleus of the tractus solitarius

Nerves

Brainstem

Tongue

Throat

Esophagus

Papillae

Microvilli

Taste buds

Nerve fibers

Taste cells

Pores

Taste buds

We all know that our appreciation of food and wine starts with our taste buds. The human tongue holds *papillae*, tiny mushroom-shaped "houses" that are located in different regions of the tongue. These houses have distinctive shapes and characteristic numbers of taste buds. Each taste bud has an opening called a pore that opens out to the surface of the tongue. The pore possesses tiny, hairlike structures known as *microvilli*. The microvilli are situated under the tissue of the tongue and they swim in our saliva. The sense receptor cells are located underneath the microvilli. Each taste receptor cell is thought to detect one type of taste. Some taste receptor cells sense sweetness, while others sense bitterness, sourness and saltiness.

Our tongues enable wine and food to come into our mouths, enter the pores, reach the receptor cells and then send a message back to our brains. While the basic taste stimuli activate the taste buds, researchers agree that other sensations—say, spicy or astringent—stimulate the mucous membranes in the mouth, as well as the taste buds. The result is, of course, pain or temperature compounded with taste.

Your "threshold" for certain tastes determines the kind of taster you are. Your threshold is defined by the lowest concentration of a basic sensation—either sourness, sweetness, bitterness or saltiness—that you can taste.

Sourness

We're born with the ability to distinguish sourness. This sour sensation tells us that a food may be spoiled and therefore could lead to illness or death, so our ability to detect this sensation is a survival mechanism. We're designed, as human beings, to relish this sensation, as well. Sourness is certainly vital in causing and experiencing a culinary orgasm. We enjoy sourness in wine and food as it creates a refreshing quality that cleans the palate and heightens and clarifies flavors. The sourness of a chilled glass of sparkling wine on a hot summer day is refreshing, pleasurable and satisfying.

Sourness in food. Sourness is a taste that pulls and contracts when inside our mouth. That's why big sourness from a food or ingredient, such as lemons, makes our mouth pucker. Sourness is a predominant taste—it always stands out. Sour foods include lemons, limes, grapefruits, fresh goat cheeses, feta, sour cream, yogurt and vinegar. Some sour-tasting ingredients partner more effectively with wines than others. White vinegar, for example, makes wine taste metallic and flat. Yet white balsamic vinegar and rice vinegar harmonize quite well with a crisp, dry white wine, such as Sauvignon Blanc or Pinot Gris. Both vinegars are less sour than a crisp, dry white wine and therefore work in partnership with it.

Sourness in wine. Wine also has acidity, experienced as sourness on our palate. Wine has three primary acids—tartaric, malic and lactic. Acidity provides the refreshing bite experienced when we sip, supports the fruit flavors and adds to the aftertaste of wine. Acidity also helps wine retain its color and preserves its lifespan. Good acidity, when balanced with other elements, will help a wine achieve a longer cellaring life. Yet a wine with too much acidity can taste too sour. This sourness is often misinterpreted as bitterness. A wine with insufficient sourness will taste flat.

Tartaric acid accounts for more than half the total acidity in wines produced in warm climates. This acid can form potassium bitartrate, glass-like crystal deposits on the cork and in the wine. The crystals, referred to as wine diamonds or wine stones, are tasteless and colorless. Wines with crystals should be decanted.

Malic acid is the sourest acid, giving wine a distinct green apple taste. It's more readily found in wines produced in cooler climates. During the wine-making process, a secondary malolactic fermentation is often employed to reduce this sour acidity and give the wine a creamy mouthfeel.

Sweetness

A newborn loves sweetness. Mother's milk is sweet. This entices the newborn to return for more, which keeps the baby healthy and well nourished. Therefore, sweetness is another survival mechanism. When sugar is placed on a pacifier and given to a baby it has a calming effect. Since we're born to love sweetness, it's a taste sensation that aids in causing a culinary orgasm.

Sweetness in food. Unlike sourness, sweetness is a pushing sensation and is the predominant taste in wine and food. It is first detected on the palate, but moves back, pushing other sensations forward, then rounds out the overall flavor of a food. Sweetness will balance heat and spice or sourness and bitterness. Consider how the sweet coconut base in red, yellow, green, Panang and Massaman curries helps to mellow the heat and spice.

Be cautious when pairing wine with sweet foods. Sweetness can clash with dry white and red wines. Many cooks like to add sugar to tomato sauce to offset the sourness of the tomatoes. Doing this balances the taste sensations in the sauce, but it also creates a problem for some dry red wines that are high in tannin and astringency. Sweetness clashes with these elements, leaving an offensive taste on the palate. If you'd like to pair tomato sauce with austere reds, use roasted tomatoes. Roasting reduces the acidity and heightens the umami in tomatoes, leaving concentrated fruitiness, deliciousness and smoky flavors that complement austere red wines. As a result, there's no need to add sugar to the sauce.

Many sugar substitutes are used today in cooking. The type of taster you are determines how you experience these substitutes. To a nontaster, the substitute called Sweet'N Low occurs as sweet. Yet, this same sugar substitute can taste offensive and bitter to a super-taster. When cooking with sugar substitutes and pairing wine to a dish, also consider the level and use of this artificial ingredient. Use it sparingly, even in desserts.

Sweetness in wine. The level of residual sugar present after fermentation defines a wine's sweetness. Sweetness makes the flavors in wine more concentrated. It also provides a sensation known as weight, or mouthfeel. It adds softness, fattiness and mellowness to wine. A wine's sweetness must be in balance with other sensations, such as sourness; otherwise, it occurs on the palate as cloying.

The perception of a wine's sweetness is often controlled by other factors, such as the level of acidity or tannin present in the wine.

This is certainly true with respect to icewine. With poor acidity, an icewine will occur as cloying and overly sweet. Yet an icewine with the same level of sweetness, but with balanced acidity (sourness), will possess clear, heightened fruit flavors and taste refreshing and palatable.

While sweet wines were once only enjoyable to the novice drinker, they're now popular among veterans, as well, due to our love affair with hot and spicy ethnic cuisines. Sweet wines are the ideal partner for the heat and spice found in Thai, East Indian and Chinese foods. Many of the world's finest wines have balanced residual sugar—they include icewines and wines from Sauternes, Barsac and Tokaj.

Sugar is present in wine in many forms. The primary and most important ones are glucose and fructose. These are fermentable sugars. If these sugars are not converted to alcohol during fermentation the resulting wine will be sweet. Other elements, by-products of fermentation, give wine sweetness. They are alcohol, glycerine and some minerals that combine with organic acids. Glycerol is a sugar alcohol and a by-product formed during the fermentation process. It's colorless and odorless, but adds softness and weight. Glycerol enhances the ripeness of fruit flavors. It's difficult to detect glycerol in wine as it takes a background role and fuses with other elements, such as sweetness and/or alcohol.

Bitterness

The detection of bitterness is, like sourness, important to our survival. Most poisons are bitter. That's why most medicines are bitter, as they're generally poisons taken in controlled doses. Bitterness does not push or pull other flavors. It's often a pleasant, lingering aftertaste in wines and foods. The bitter aftertaste in fresh herbs, for example, creates a wholeness in our tasting experience. For this reason, bitterness certainly contributes, like sourness and sweetness, to the harmony of both wine and food and their overall partnership. Bitterness is a necessary component when you're striving for a culinary orgasm.

Bitterness in food. Scientists now know that there are about five bitter tastes, although they don't yet have scientific names for them. We do know that the bitterness of cured olives occurs differently on our palate than the bitterness found in the skin of a walnut. Watercress is bitter. Fresh herbs like rosemary are bitter. Almonds have some bitterness, as do radicchio, spinach and some beers. The kind of taster you are also determines how much bitterness you find pleasant before you start to find it offensive.

Bitterness in wine. In wine, the basic taste of bitterness usually appears in partnership with the secondary taste of astringency. It's often confused with sourness in wine. Sourness gives your mouth a puckering effect. The bitterness and astringency in wine create a cheek-drying quality inside the mouth, similar to the experience of brewed tea, quality coffee or walnuts. Bitterness lingers on the palate as an aftertaste.

Phenols play a role in wine's color, its taste (bitterness and astringency) and weight. The phenol levels help determine the taste differences between and health benefits of white and red wines. Tannin is the name given to phenolic compounds that come from the stems, skins and seeds of grapes. Phenolic compounds in wine can also derive from the oak barrels used for fermentation and aging. Tannin levels are determined by many factors, such as:

- the grape variety used in the making of a particular wine
- the duration of skin/stem contact before and during fermentation
- the severity of the pressing of juice from the grapes
- the time spent in an oak barrel

Sur lie is a French term that means "on the lees." This is the process of aging wine on its deposit of dead yeast and grape particles after the primary fermentation. This process adds bitterness and astringency, as well as toasty aromas, weight/body and stability. When yeast cells die, their cell walls break down, gradually releasing compounds into the wine. These compounds include polysaccharides (e.g., glucose), amino acids and fatty acids. These released compounds influence the structural integration of the wine in terms of its weight, tannin, aroma and stability.

Saltiness

We're born with the ability to distinguish and crave salt. We might otherwise die as a result of salt depletion. Our nerves and muscles require it to function. So we crave salt as a survival mechanism. Quality salt, when consumed in moderation, is actually good for us.

Saltiness in food. There's nothing more sexy and satisfying than the sea-brininess of fresh oysters on the half shell. Saltiness in food can easily become addictive, especially to nontasters.

Many kinds of salt exist. For cooking and for health, I prefer sea salt. Refined and processed salt is clean and sparkling, but is said to be missing the minerals and trace elements that once made salt so valuable. Quality sea salt is high in both, is natural and tastes better.

Many countries produce sea salt. Wales produces Halen Mon, a sea salt hand-harvested from Atlantic waters. *Fleur de sel*, meaning "flower of salt," comes from the island of Ré, off France's Atlantic coast. Since the seventh century, the sun and wind have evaporated the seawater there, leaving fine crystals that are harvested by hand in July and August. Fleur de sel is recognized for its delicate flavor and concentration of minerals and trace elements. This quality sea salt doesn't bite the tip of the tongue like refined table salt. It's best used as a condiment, where its finest qualities, such as its delicate flavor and texture, will shine through.

Celtic gray sea salt is another product of France, and comes from the coastal marshes of Brittany. It was once a well-kept secret, highly regarded by chefs around the world. Celtic gray sea salt is more widely available today and is now reasonably priced. Britain, New Zealand, Australia and Hawaii all produce their own salts from the sea, as well.

Saltiness in wine. Wine contains the salts of mineral acids and a few organic acids. Potassium bitartrate has both an acid and a salty taste. Wines rarely have a salty taste, although some Portuguese and Fanagoria wines, due to the local soils, may seem slightly salty. Some Australian wines are also believed to have a higher level of chloride, due to their terroir. Chloride is one of the components that make up table salt. Nevertheless, saltiness in general should be undetectable in well-made wines.

SECONDARY TASTE SENSATIONS

While the basic tastes of sweetness, sourness, bitterness and saltiness activate the taste buds, there are other sensations that stimulate the mucous membrane in the mouth. These secondary sensations are spiciness, metallic-ness and astringency.

Heat and Spice

Substances like ethanol and capsaicin are chemosensory irritations. They cause a burning sensation by inducing a trigeminal nerve reaction together with normal taste reception. Lovers of oysters on the half shell often add Tabasco sauce to increase the pleasure of the mouthfeel. Chemosensory irritation is an integral element in our flavor perception of the foods of Mexico, India, China, Korea, Indonesia, Vietnam and Thailand.

Hot and spicy foods can elicit an endorphin rush. The term "endorphin rush" refers to feelings of exhilaration brought on by pain, danger or other forms of stress. People who enjoy lots of spicy capsaicin-rich foods can build up a tolerance to it. A large jolt of capsaicin excites the nervous system into producing endorphins, which promotes a sense of well-being. It's a rush that can become addictive. It's also a rush that the excessive nontaster may consider orgasmic.

Metallic Taste

Certain wine and food combinations will create a metallic taste on the palate. When wine is paired with dishes highlighting certain vinegars, such as white or cider, a metallic taste is produced. Wine must be at least as sour as the acid ingredient being used within the appetizer. Acetic acid is more sour than wine and this is why the metallic taste emerges.

Foods such as seaweed, artichokes and asparagus, when paired with some wines, can also create a metallic taste on the palate. For example, asparagus and red wine are not great friends and certainly won't be the source of a culinary orgasm. Such ingredients can be paired with white wines, as long as other elements are added.

Astringency

For avid wine lovers, astringency is a sensation enjoyed in partnership with bitterness. In both wine and food, astringency comes from tannin. We also taste astringency when we eat under-ripe fruits. We experience astringency as a rough sensation on the teeth. People consider it pleasant in beverages and foods, such as wine, tea, rhubarb, grapes, walnuts and bananas. Astringency also heightens other flavors. That's why red wines high in tannin and astringency don't work well with hot and spicy food. The tannin and astringency increase the perception of heat. Other terms for astringency are "dry," "rough," "harsh" and "hard." The Tea-Infused Dark Chocolate Truffles (page 214) are an example of an appetizer that celebrates the partnership of bitterness (from the cocoa) and astringency (from the tea infusion), sensations that harmonize with dry red wine and port.

the *building block principles*

For my teaching and client appreciation events, I created a system called The Building Block Principles to help wine lovers partner wine with food consistently and effectively. These same principles apply to the pairings in this book.

What are building blocks? I define the building blocks of wine and food as the tastes and flavors that human beings can readily identify. We also crave these universal sensations on a daily basis in our North American diet. They're the blocks that build a wine and food partnership, the source of the amplified experience I refer to as a culinary orgasm.

These tangible and identifiable tastes and flavors—building blocks—are:

- Sourness
- Sweetness
- Fruitiness
- Bitterness
- Saltiness
- Heat and spiciness
- Fattiness (see page 27)

We're all familiar with these sensations when they appear in food. But sometimes it's more challenging to identify sourness, sweetness, bitterness, fruitiness and fattiness in wine. A particular wine's predominant building blocks are the key factors that determine the "style" in which the wine has been made. When it comes to pairing wine with food or vice versa, the wine's style should be considered first, before its origin or grape variety. The style includes its origin or region, its terroir, its grape variety and the wine-making practices employed in making it.

This chart maps out the wine styles I consider to be the most popular and their predominant building blocks.

WINE STYLES AND PREDOMINANT BUILDING BLOCKS

wine style	*sourness*	*sweetness*	*fruitiness*	*bitterness*	*fattiness*
dry sparkling	*		*	some	
off-dry sparkling	*	some	*		
crisp, dry white	*		*	some	
well-balanced, medium-bodied, smooth white	*		*		some
big, fat white	some		some	some	*
off-dry white	*	some	*		
off-dry rosé	*	some	*		
dry rosés and light fruit reds	*		*	some	
reds with forward fruit	some		*	some	*
austere reds	some		some	*	*
late harvest and icewines	*	*	*		*
dry port and port-style	*	*	*	some	*
sweet port and port-style		*	*	some	*

The three principles below describe the essential rules for pairing wine with food. Once you know them by heart, you'll be able to utilize these principles to create more layered and sophisticated partnerships. No matter the apparent difficulty of a recipe or the challenges its ethnic influence may offer, any dish can be deconstructed down to its basic Building Block Principles.

PRINCIPLE ONE: PAIR SAME WITH SAME

Pair the building blocks in the wine to the same building blocks in the food. Pair sourness with sourness. Pair the sourness of goat cheese with the sourness of a crisp, dry white wine. The same holds true for all the building block sensations. Pair:

- sweet wine with sweet food (dark chocolate and port)

- bitter wine with bitter food (olive tapenade pizza with austere red wine)

- fatty wine with fatty food (big, fat white with an Alfredo sauce over pasta)

- fruity wine with fruity food (red wine with forward fruitiness with fruity roasted red peppers or roasted tomatoes)

PRINCIPLE TWO:
ONLY OFFSET WHEN NECESSARY

Offset the building blocks only when you cannot match them. It's a good idea when the food is salty or hot and spicy, for example. Since there's no such thing as salty or spicy sensations in wine, you must "offset" these sensations with a building block that already exists in wine. Salty foods harmonize with sour wines, much like salt and vinegar chips. A classic example is pairing oysters on the half shell with Sauvignon Blanc, or smoked salmon canapés with a dry Riesling. Wines with sweetness nicely offset hot and spicy foods. An off-dry Riesling or off-dry

rosé perfectly offset the heat and spice of barbecued chicken skewers with hot and spicy peanut sauce. Partner:

- salty foods with sour wines (anchovies and crisp, dry whites)

- hot and spicy foods with sweet wines (Thai coconut curry with off-dry whites)

PRINCIPLE THREE:
THE WINE'S PREDOMINANT BUILDING BLOCK SHOULD BE EQUAL TO OR GREATER THAN THE ONE IN THE FOOD

This principle applies to both the sharing of building blocks and the offsetting of them. Make sure the wine's acidity (sourness) is equal to, or greater than, the sourness in the dish. Make sure your crisp, dry white wine is more sour than the vinegar in your vinaigrette. Make sure the wine's sweetness is of equal value to, or greater than, the heat and spiciness of a dish. This applies to all the building blocks. If the dish possesses more of the predominant sensation than the wine, the wine will taste nondescript and flat. If your wine tastes flat and vanishes alongside the dish you've paired with it, you might as well drink water.

- Good Pairing: Crisp, dry white with rice vinegar (they harmonize because the wine is more sour than the vinegar)

- Poor Pairing: Crisp, dry white with white vinegar (the result is an offensive metallic taste because this particular vinegar is more sour than the wine)

- Good Pairing: Icewine with fresh fruit (they harmonize because the wine is sweeter than the fruit)

- Poor Pairing: Icewine with milk chocolate (the result is an acidic and metallic taste because the chocolate is sweeter than the icewine)

Every wine has more than one building block. The food and wine pairing wheel below features the predominant wine styles and some of their best food matches. It celebrates the most popular varietal wines consumed today and only a few of the hundreds of partnership possibilities.

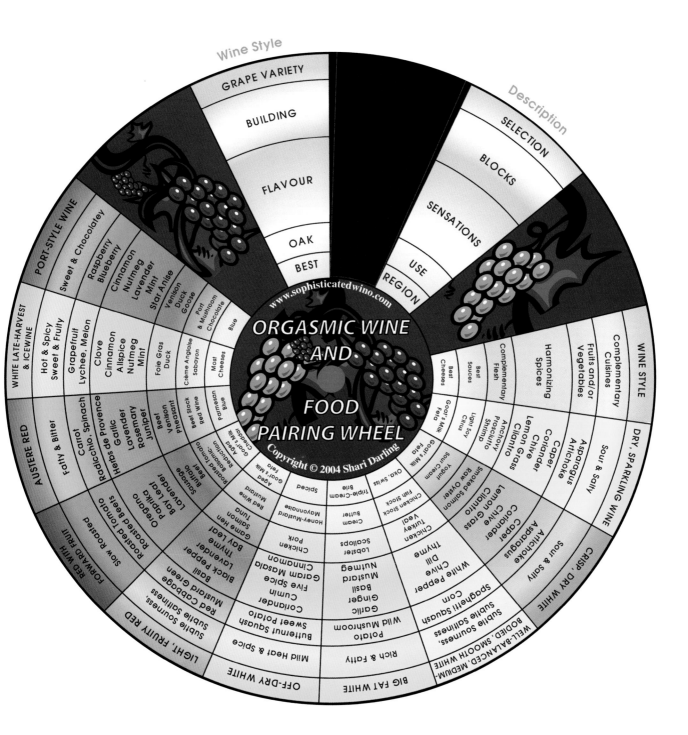

WHAT KIND OF TASTER ARE YOU?

Each of us has a unique palate, but we fall into one of three groups of tasters: super-tasters, medium-tasters and nontasters. One group is not better than the others. Your genetically determined number of taste receptors is responsible for the kind of taster you are and the sorts of foods and wines you enjoy. Gender also enters into the equation. About 35 percent of females are considered super-tasters, while only 10 percent of males belong to this group. New research also shows that ethnic groups differ and that, for instance, there are more super-tasting Asians and Africans than Caucasians. The cause of this heightened taste sensitivity among certain ethnic groups is still unknown.

Super-tasters account for 25 percent of the population; they possess a highly sensitive palate. They experience the taste, temperature and texture of foods, most specifically bitterness, more keenly than the other tasters. To the super-taster, espresso, olives, arugula, dark chocolate and dry whites can taste too bitter and are therefore not palatable. Super-tasters experience intense tastes and oral burns from chemical irritants such as chili peppers, black pepper and cayenne. They also perceive the most intense sensations from salt, acids and sweeteners, as well as fats in foods.

Medium-tasters make up about 50 percent of the population, while nontasters account for about 25 percent.

The kind of taster you are therefore influences the wines and foods you enjoy. Knowing this allows you to be sensitive to other people's taste preferences, especially when you're cooking for others or buying wine as a gift. The wine you find exceptional because you're a

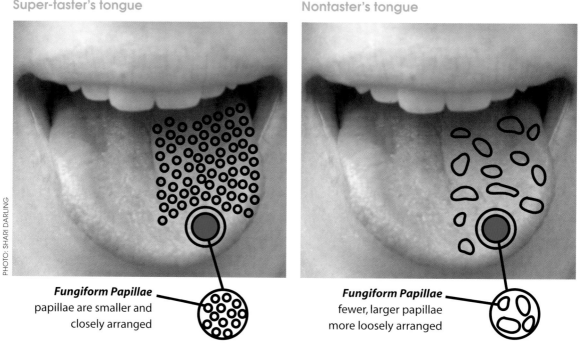

Super-taster's tongue

Nontaster's tongue

PHOTO: SHARI DARLING

Fungiform Papillae papillae are smaller and closely arranged

Fungiform Papillae fewer, larger papillae more loosely arranged

Notice the difference in the number, size and shape of taste buds between a super-taster's tongue (left) and a nontaster's (right).

nontaster may be considered unacceptable to your super-tasting romantic partner.

I'm a nontaster. I love smelly blue cheese, an entire bulb (not a clove) of garlic in my spaghetti sauce and wines with "in your face" character. But when I'm entertaining, I make a conscious choice to reduce the salt content of my dishes, knowing I'll no doubt have medium- and super-tasters dining at the table.

I'm a huge fan of grappa. Grappa is a pomace brandy of about 30 to 80 percent alcohol; it's high in antioxidants and therefore is a great digestive after a heavy meal. It's made from grape residue, the last bit of wine left in the skins, stems and stalks after the first and second pressing of the grapes. The flavor of grappa depends on the type and quality of the grapes used, as well the specifics of the distillation process.

As a nontaster, I prefer the rather harsh, bitter versions. The super-taster, however, would no doubt find this lovely beverage to be far too bitter and offensive. Today, grappa is also being made from the first pressing of grapes. This process allows the resulting spirit to be much smoother, with little bitterness. Super-tasters may want to seek out these versions.

In *Harmony on the Palate*, I provide an experiment to help you determine the kind of taster you are. But you need only look at your current diet, your likes and dislikes, to know what group you probably fit into. Do you like young mozzarella or stinky blue cheese? Do you drink your coffee with double cream and sugar, or black and sugarless? Are the wines you enjoy gentle and smooth, or edgy with loads of sourness or bitterness?

Who's your umami?

Potato chips and french fries are addictive. One potato chip, like one french fry, is never enough to satisfy our desire. These snacks, along with spaghetti and meatballs, are considered umami-rich foods. Umami is an important sensation that contributes to the culinary orgasm.

Umami (pronounced *oo-MA-mee*) is the Japanese word for savoriness. It's now internationally recognized as a legitimate fifth taste sensation, alongside sweetness, sourness, saltiness and bitterness. Scientists have discovered that a mother's milk is not just sweet, but also high in glutamate—umami—which tells us that this sensation is as vital to our survival as the other four. Breast milk contains 21.6 mg per 100 mL of glutamate. Our subconscious need for umami actually supports a whole array of biological needs, including our appetite for the protein-rich foods we use as metabolic fuel. The primary substances that offer this fifth taste are glutamate (an amino acid) and ribonucleotides.

BASIC UMAMI

Glutamate stimulates tired taste buds and olfactory nerve endings. It's also good for our digestive tract. There are two forms of glutamate: "bound" and "free." Bound glutamate is linked to protein; free glutamate is not.

Foods containing glutamate possess the basic umami taste. Glutamate gives the umami flavor to an array of ingredients, such as ripe tomatoes, cured meats (aged beef) and cheeses such as Parmigiano-Reggiano. It also lends umami to fermented seasonings, such as Asian fish sauce and Japanese miso paste.

SYNERGISTIC UMAMI

The term *synergy*, according to the *Oxford Dictionary*, means "the interaction or cooperation of two or more agents to produce a combined effect greater than the sum of their separate effects." When foods with glutamate undergo a further culinary process—such as slow cooking, fermentation or aging—the enzymatic action breaks down the ribonucleotides. The perceived strength of the umami taste is substantially increased, adding up to more than the sum of its separate substances. The experts and scientists of the Umami Information Center in Tokyo, Japan, call this the "synergistic effect" of umami. Although scientists don't yet fully understand why this occurs, Japanese chefs have been utilizing this culinary miracle for centuries.

To the North American palate, this fifth taste sensation may seem mysterious and indefinable, but it's not. We're subconsciously addicted to umami in forms such as ketchup. Thai cuisine highlights the fermented fish sauce, *nam pla*, which is high in umami. Marmite is another umami-rich food that many Brits like to spread on toast. People around the globe enjoy Italy's Parmigiano-Reggiano.

This umami map pinpoints a few of the world's most umami-rich foods.

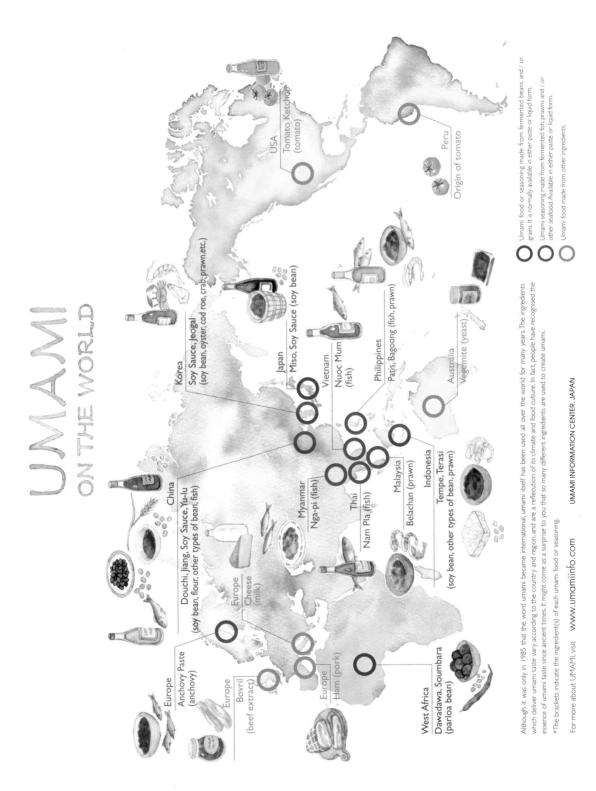

UMAMI
ON THE WORLD

USA
Tomato Ketchup
(tomato)

Peru
Origin of tomato

Korea
Soy Sauce, Jeogal
(soy bean, oyster, cod roe, crab, prawn, etc.)

Japan
Miso, Soy Sauce (soy bean)

Vietnam
Nuoc Mum
(fish)

Philippines
Patis, Bagoong (fish, prawn)

Australia
Vegemite (yeast)

China
Douchi, Jiang, Soy Sauce, Yu-lu
(soy bean, flour, other types of bean, fish)

Myanmar
Nga-pi (fish)

Thai
Nam Pla (fish)

Malaysia
Belachan (prawn)

Indonesia
Tempe, Terasi
(soy bean, other types of bean, prawn)

Europe
Cheese
(milk)

Europe
Anchovy Paste
(anchovy)

Europe
Bovril
(beef extract)

Europe
Ham (pork)

West Africa
Dawadawa, Soumbara
(parloa bean)

Umami food or seasoning made from fermented beans and / or grains. It is normally available in either paste or liquid form.

Umami seasoning made from fermented fish, prawns and / or other seafood. Available in either paste or liquid form.

Umami food made from other ingredients.

Although it was only in 1985 that the word umami became international, umami itself has been used all over the world for many years. The ingredients which deliver umami taste vary according to the country and region, and are a reflection of its climate and food culture. In fact, people have recognised the essence of umami taste since ancient times. It might come as a surprise to you that so many different ingredients are used to create umami.

*The brackets indicate the ingredient(s) of each umami food or seasoning.

For more about UMAMI, visit   www.umamiinfo.com   UMAMI INFORMATION CENTER, JAPAN

Some of the preparations, processes and cooking techniques that create synergistic umami are:

- the ripening process (Parmesan)
- fermentation (soy sauce)
- slow cooking (bouillon, tomato sauce)
- steaming (potatoes, asparagus)
- dry aging (aged beef)
- drying or dehydrating
- dry curing (bacon)
- fermentation/pickling (though not pickling alone)

YOUR SECRET WEAPON

Understanding basic and synergistic umami gives you the power to use its potency in the preparation of your appetizers. It can be the secret weapon in transforming a simple appetizer into an appetizer with the MOAN FACTOR. When added to a dish, umami provides amplitude and continuity—enhancement, roundness, depth of flavor and heightened flavor.

Umami enhances flavor. Chowder and bisque served in a shot glass are fabulous appetizers to serve on cold winter evenings, especially over the holidays. Lobster bisque combines lobster, potatoes and cream. You can enhance these flavors by adding basic and synergistic umami ingredients like shiitake mushrooms (basic) and dry sherry (synergistic). These ingredients dramatically enhance the flavor of your bisque.

Umami layers flavor. Umami also allows for different flavors in an appetizer to peak at various times during the eating experience. A perfect example is the addition of freshly grated Parmigiano-Reggiano (synergistic) over a simple tomato bruschetta. The addition of this cheese creates a yummy flourish to your bruschetta experience. Condiments such as Worcestershire sauce are often served along-

side steak. That's because such sauces provide another layer of synergistic umami to a simple cut of fresh or aged beef.

Umami adds depth of flavor. Beef skewers seasoned with salt and pepper and grilled on the barbecue are simple and tasty. But to increase this appetizer's orgasmic quality, use thin slices of aged beef marinated in soy sauce, dry sherry, sesame oil and garlic. Aged beef, soy sauce and dry sherry are umami-rich and add depth of flavor. Fortified wines like sherry and port undergo aging and therefore contain synergistic umami, as well. The addition of anchovies to a Caesar salad dressing is an example of how umami adds a depth of flavor to an otherwise two-dimensional combination of tastes.

Umami heightens flavor and rounds out flavor. Umami-addicted and umami-conscious chefs keep a supply of Asian fish sauce on hand to use as a secret weapon in their marinades, salad dressings and sauces. Fish may or may not be included in the resulting dish. Fish sauce is a fermented product that's high in synergistic umami. Adding it rounds out the flavors in any dish.

Explore Umami in Wine

While the subject of umami occurring in wine is still being explored by chefs, scientists, winemakers and sommeliers, a few facts regarding the presence of umami in wine have become apparent. White wines don't develop as much umami as reds. Unlike reds, white wines are meant to be consumed within two years of being purchased. The cellaring process "ages" the wine, increasing its umami taste. Aged red wines often have earthy tones.

Pair Wines with Umami-Rich Appetizers

Umami need not be considered as a primary building block when pairing wine with food. You should certainly consider the predominant building blocks of sweet, sour, salty, bitter, fatty and fruity when you're trying to create a harmonious partnership. However, umami-rich foods, such as aged beef, Parmigiano-Reggiano, ripened brie and black and white truffles often have an earthy character. I personally like to consider this earthiness when hunting for an appropriate wine.

UMAMI FOOD CHARTS

The Basic Umami Chart lists umami-rich foods to help you make orgasmic appetizers from scratch. The list is by no means complete; it contains only some of the countless umami-rich ingredients to consider, a few of which scientists are still debating in terms of their umami content.

basic umami chart

tubers: potatoes, winter squash

vegetables: asparagus, spinach, bell peppers

grains: corn, rice

legumes: kidney beans, navy beans, lentils, lima beans, peas

sea vegetables: kombu, nori, kelp

beef: brisket, shanks, chuck, steak

poultry: duck, turkey

game: venison

fish: anchovy, salmon, tuna, sardines, bluefish

shellfish: oyster, scallop, lobster, shrimp, crab

fungi: shiitake, portobello, morels, porcini

truffles: white, black

synergistic umami chart

cheese: Parmesan, Romano, brie, cheddar, gouda

cured: bacon, cured ham, prosciutto, Spanish serrano

fermented/pickled: kosher dills, sauerkraut, kimchi, black olives, pickled ginger

soy: steamed or stir-fried tofu, soy sauce, tempeh, natto, miso

condiments: fish sauce, fish pastes, Worcestershire sauce, ketchup

fermented/brewed/distilled: sherry, Madeira, port, sake, whisky

UMAMI HISTORY

About a hundred years ago a Japanese scientist named Professor Kikunae Ikeda recognized a common factor within the intricate flavors of certain foods such as asparagus, ripe tomatoes, cheese and aged meat. This factor could not be identified as sour, sweet, salty or bitter. After much scientific research and investigation, Ikeda discovered that the taste was produced by glutamate, called "umami" in Japanese. Intrigued by the distinctive and easily identifiable flavors of kombu, a dried seaweed used for over a thousand years in Japanese soups and stocks, he investigated further. Ikeda decided to call the flavor he had isolated "umami." In 1909, Ikeda developed a product based on the concept of umami, called monosodium glutamate (MSG). Partly as a result of this, Professor Ikeda has been listed as one of the ten greatest Japanese inventors of all time.

Interestingly, before this discovery, a Swiss flour manufacturer, Julius Magi, had created a commercially viable product called "bouillon cubes" in 1882. Since meat was too expensive for many families, these cubes were sold to flavor soups. At the time, Magi did not know his bouillon cubes were based on the premise of umami. We've come to crave umami in its basic and synergistic forms in our indigenous foods, the prepared foods we buy and in our multicultural cuisine. Using umami-rich foods will certainly give your appetizers the MOAN FACTOR.

the *Sense of flavor*

While we may crave certain taste sensations that are necessary to our survival, we also relish the layers of flavor in quality wine and food. We detect the most important element of flavor through our noses, a process called orthonasal olfaction, and through the inside of our mouths, retronasal olfaction.

AROMAS

We think we love the taste of chocolate, but what we actually cherish are the sweet and bitter sensations it produces, accompanied by its wonderful cocoa aromas. That's why chocolate experts insist that we rub the chocolate with our fingers to release its aromas, then smell it and then suck on it, to savor these aromas from inside the mouth.

The smells of wine and food are registered in our brain by the olfactory epithelium. The epithelium tissue sits inside the nasal cavity (about one inch wide and two inches long) and lies on the roof of the nasal cavity, about three inches above and behind the nostrils. The olfactory epithelium is the part of the olfactory system directly responsible for detecting odors. Aromas enter through the fine hairs of the nose and progress to the limbic system, the part of the brain that controls our moods, emotions, memory and learning. Our sense of smell is ten thousand times stronger than our other senses. That's why it's an integral element in experiencing a culinary orgasm.

We're not born with an understanding of aromas. We develop our likes and dislikes for them during childhood and our brain stores our emotions and memories of them.

Aromas in Wine

Wine is highly aromatic, so it stimulates our sense of smell and therefore our emotions and memories. For this reason you can add another dimension of culinary pleasure to your evening by taking your guests through a fun and informal tasting of the wines you have on hand. Before stimulating their sense of smell, have your guests look at the wine in their glass. The style of wine being served can be enough to create or transform the mood of an event. Champagne, for example, sets the tone for a celebration. Red wines can make us feel comfortable and relaxed. The color of a wine also stimulates our sense of sight and adventure. This is discussed in further detail on page 30.

But back to aromas: Direct each of your guests to swirl the wine within the bowl of their glass and then stick their nose in to take a gentle sniff. The art of "nosing" the wine lies in being able to identify its aromas and articulate them. The discussion of aromas can be an intimate affair. At the same time as we are experiencing the wine in a roomful of people, we form our own personal impressions of it. Two people can smell the same wine and experience completely different aromas.

In other words, there is no right way to describe the "nose" and flavors of a wine.

Whenever I smell an off-dry rosé, for instance, I feel happy and excited, open and ready to play. Rosés with this hint of sweetness smell like candy apples to me, immediately taking me back to my childhood. Every summer, my mom would take my siblings and me to the Canadian National Exhibition to enjoy the roller coaster and games. We were allowed to indulge in one cotton candy and one candy apple per summer. (My mother closely monitored our intake of sugar to reduce the risk of cavities and therefore expensive fillings.) Today, the scent of candy apples in an off-dry rosé still tickles my fancy!

Show your guests how to "aerate" the wine. This means, after sipping, you let the wine fall to the inside surface of your lips and then whistle backward. This brings air into your mouth, releasing the wine's aromas. The aromas are then carried back up through the olfactory canal. Have your guests "chew" the wine, as well. Chewing is like gurgling, swishing the wine in the mouth, making sure it touches every corner and crevice, even inside the inner top lip. Chewing is performed to experience and fully appreciate the wine's taste sensations. Remember, everyone has a unique palate, with varying numbers of taste buds in different areas. Chewing ensures that you will get the full pleasure of the wine's sensations, whatever kind of taster you are.

The last step for you and your fellow tasters is to assess the wine's "finish," which means identifying how long the wine lasts on the palate after it has been swallowed. Like great coffee, the longer a wine lasts on the palate after swallowing, the better its quality. The term "falling short" means the wine evaporates from the palate the moment it's swallowed.

Aromas in Food

There are few smells more tantalizing than the yeasty aroma of baking pastries, the smell of sizzling bacon or the pungent scent of roasting garlic. These comfort food aromas are enough to start anyone salivating, setting them up for culinary bliss.

While they stimulate the appetite and prepare the palate for a gastronomic adventure, aromatic hot appetizers interfere with the aromas and flavors of wine. So be sure to build or layer the scents and tastes in the room throughout the evening of your event. Before placing your hot appetizers in the oven, be sure your guests have had the opportunity to smell and sample the chilled and room-temperature treats. After a while, place the hot ones in the oven, creating another dimension of aromas to stimulate their sense of smell as the evening progresses.

Orthonasal and Retronasal Aromas

When pairing wine to appetizers, the orthonasal and retronasal smells of both are important. While there are literally thousands of aromas in wine and food, there are some familiar ones you'll want to consider.

Vinted. Wine lovers often use wine as an ingredient when cooking. A splash of white wine in macaroni and cheese moves it from a simple comfort food to layered gourmet fare. Besides its aromatics, wine as an ingredient also provides taste sensations, such as sourness (acidity) and fruitiness. The alcohol in wine evaporates during the cooking process, so it doesn't contribute any aromas, viscosity or weight to the dish. As an ingredient, red wine adds some bitterness (taste sensation) and concentrated fruitiness (flavor). It's also a great flesh tenderizer.

Fruitiness. Oranges, lemons, limes and peaches are highly aromatic in bite-sized desserts. So, too, are fruits of every kind when used in savory dishes. Barbecued baby back ribs basted with caramelized raspberry preserves are highly aromatic. Every fruit has its basic taste sensations, such as sour (cranberries), sweet (coconut) and bitter (the pits of raspberries), as well as specific fruity aromas and flavors. When pairing appetizers that incorporate fruit to specific wines, both the taste sensations and aromatics (flavors) must be considered.

A dollop of applesauce on a mini sweet potato latke adds sweetness and apple flavors. A Chardonnay can offer apple flavors, as well. Yet this doesn't mean the applesauce will harmonize with a Chardonnay. Remember the Building Block Principles. Applesauce has a predominant building block of sweetness, while the wine's primary building block is sourness. Applesauce and Chardonnay clash, as do fresh apples and Chardonnay. In building block terms, sourness in wine clashes with sweetness in food. An off-dry Riesling with sweetness, on the other hand, tastes fabulous when paired with applesauce and fresh apples. Even if the off-dry Riesling has apricot or dried raisin flavors, it still shares the same building block of sweetness as is found in applesauce and apples. Hence it's an ideal partnership.

THE AROMATIC TRIO

You can create complex flavors when you combine aromatic vegetables, aromatic herbs and ingredients high in umami.

Many fabulous appetizers feature aromatic vegetables. Onions, leeks, fennel and carrots are great examples, as they're all highly aromatic when slow-roasted, sautéed or caramelized in fat. Aromatic vegetables are the foundation of many orgasmic appetizers. Truffle Mashed Potatoes with Garlic & Caramelized Leeks (page 182) exemplifies this idea. Soups, stews and chowders incorporating this aromatic trio can be served as taste tantalizers in shot glasses.

The French use aromatic vegetables as a flavor foundation for soups, stews and sauces. Their classic combination, the *mirepoix*, is made up of twice as many onions as carrots and celery. The vegetables are diced, helping them cook more evenly and quickly. Just as the French make *mirepoix*, the Italians create *soffritto* and the Portuguese have *refogado*.

Aromatic Vegetables with Wine

Aromatic vegetables are also highly flavorful. When onions, leeks and carrots are slow-roasted or caramelized, their sugars concentrate. The predominant building block here is sweetness, which should be considered when you're choosing a complementary wine. Choose a white with some sweetness, such as an off-dry Riesling or off-dry Gewürztraminer. Stick with reds highlighting forward fruit character and low tannin, such as Merlot. The bitterness and dryness (tannin and astringency) in austere reds will clash with the sweetness in slow-roasted and caramelized vegetables.

Aromatic Herbs

Aromatic herbs are often incorporated into flavor bases like *mirepoix*. They're green and leafy, like basil, rosemary, oregano and thyme. Combining aromatic vegetables or ingredients high in umami with aromatic herbs helps imbue appetizers with the MOAN FACTOR. Caramelized Onion, Rosemary & Stilton Flatbread (page 162) uses the aromatic vegetable, onion, with the aromatic herb, rosemary. Tomatoes are high in umami and sing with flavor when combined with the aroma, taste and flavor of basil. In Indonesian cooking, galangal and kemiri are often combined with shrimp paste to create a flavor base. Galangal and kemiri are aromatic. Shrimp paste is high in umami. Thai cuisine incorporates curry paste (an umami ingredient) with lemongrass and kaffir lime leaves.

Aromatic herbs with wine

Depending on the cuisine and cooking method used, aromatic herbs can complement wine. Different herbs harmonize with specific grape varieties, in fact. (See the Orgasmic Food and Wine Pairing Wheel on page 15.) Remember that the incorporation of aromatic herbs in an appetizer is usually an element of artistic expression. Be sure to first consider the predominant building blocks in the dish alongside those in the wine.

By the same token, an aromatic herb can take center stage in an appetizer and be the featured harmonizing ingredient, as long as the building blocks in both work well together. Baby lamb chops coated in olive oil and seasoned with salt, pepper and fresh rosemary taste sublime when partnered with a red wine that has forward fruitiness, such as Merlot or Shiraz. The fattiness in a red with forward fruit works with the fattiness of lamb. So, the partners share the first building block principle. However, rosemary assumes the main role in this appetizer. (See page 166.) Through roasting, fresh rosemary becomes intensely fruity, thus complementing the fruity character of this velvety red. Fresh basil and oregano offer both strong color and forward flavor in an appetizer like Mini Treasures (page 73), as well.

Cooking with freshly picked herbs from my garden is one of my greatest summertime pleasures. Even if you don't have a garden of your own, you can still indulge in the pleasure of cooking with fresh herbs. Most supermarkets carry a wide selection. Whenever possible, use fresh herbs instead of the dried variety for appetizer recipes and garnishes. While dried versions are more concentrated, fresh herbs are highly aromatic and add incredible color and subtle flavors to almost any dish, including appetizers. I like to arrange fresh oregano leaves over tomato sauce on simple tomato and cheese pizzettas. My husband loves homemade herb pesto on bruschetta. To make the pesto, I pick a variety of herbs, toss them into the blender with garlic, olive oil and pine nuts or walnuts and presto! I have a highly aromatic, fresh herb pesto in less than a minute. Of course, the primary component in any pesto is olive oil. This means you can marry herb pestos with wines offering lots of fattiness. Look for wines with plenty of alcohol in them, about 13 to 14 percent. The higher the alcohol content, the oilier the wine's mouthfeel.

Many herbs complement specific ingredients. Basil and tomato, rosemary and brie, mint and lamb are but a few examples of herbs and foods that go hand in hand. (See the chapter Tantric Twosomes and Titillating Trios.) Appetizers using chicken, turkey and duck all benefit from the addition of marjoram, sage and thyme. Fresh sage and thyme have a pleasant bitterness. This building block complements the bitterness in austere red wines.

Due to their strong aromas and flavors, chives, dill and lemongrass work nicely with a variety of seafood. Brut sparkling wines and crisp, dry whites are their best matches.

Basil, marjoram and oregano tend to go with heavier appetizers that highlight cream and therefore complement big, fat whites. Oregano, rosemary and thyme are flavorful herbs for beef-, lamb-, duck- and venison-based dishes. Keep in mind that the herbs you choose should also reflect the ethnic style of your appetizer. Lemongrass and kaffir lime leaves are an integral element in Thai cuisine, while Middle Eastern dishes can incorporate parsley and mint.

Aromatic Spices

Spices such as cinnamon, cardamom and allspice provide both aromatics and undertones to appetizers. Due to their aromatics, they can easily dominate the flavors of a dish. Use them sparingly. Aromatic spices are meant to be subtle and intriguing, adding a gentle undercurrent of flavor. A pinch of cinnamon goes a long way in adding sweet and bitter tastes, richness and spicy aromas to jerk seasoning and even to baked apples.

Spiciness with wine

Be cautious when pairing wine to appetizers highlighting aromatic spices. Is the spice part of a flavor combination intended to add subtle flavor to an appetizer? Or is the spice or spice blend the primary source of flavor? A pinch of cinnamon and allspice in a mini apple tart acts as subtle support for the primary building block of sweetness in the apples. The sweetness is of interest when finding the appropriate wine partner.

Sometimes, though, the spice combination is the focus of the appetizer. Blackened oysters, for example, highlight Cajun seasoning (see page 49 for a recipe). This hot and spicy coating, more than the oyster itself, must be considered when choosing a wine. Jerk and Cajun seasonings combine many spices, but share the predominant building block of hot and spicy. This heat (not temperature) can destroy the qualities of a fabulous wine, if not properly considered. Gentle curry, for example, can work nicely with a red wine with forward fruit, such as Merlot or Shiraz. Yet, a hot, spicy curry clashes with red wine. It will taste hotter when partnered with austere reds possessing decent to heavy tannin. Hot and spicy dishes ultimately work best with wines offering some sweetness. Remember the third Building Block Principle— make sure the wine contains sweetness that is equal to or more than the heat and spice of the dish.

Many spices have a natural affinity to specific wine styles. Lemongrass is sour, lemony and fresh and so works nicely with brut sparkling wines and crisp, dry whites. Fennel is highly aromatic and sweet with licorice tones

that complement wines in the styles of off-dry whites, off-dry rosés and dessert wines. Juniper is bitter and slightly sweet, a highly complementary spice when paired with austere reds.

Funky and Musty

Nontasters, more than medium- and supertasters, tend to enjoy funky, stinky and musty aromas and flavors in wine and food. In fact, there's nothing more delightful to a nontaster than the opportunity to taste a funky brie, on the edge of over-ripening, on garlic toasts, paired with a red wine emphasizing its Brett character (see sidebar on facing page). This category of taster, I believe, appears to savor umami-rich foods, such as dried mushrooms, aged cheeses like brie and Parmigiano-Reggiano, dry aged beef and cured ham.

In the umami-rich group, you'll also find truffles. White truffles are more aromatic than black ones. Some experts say their smell comes from their level of sulfur compounds. Over time this smell becomes more mushroom-like. Or, as a true truffle aficionado might say, "They have aromas of sweet, wild garlic with Parmigiano-Reggiano, added honey, spices, tree bark and a whiff of earthy mushroom." And while there's no tangible evidence, truffles are considered an aphrodisiac—at least, to a truffle fan.

"Whoever says 'truffle' utters a great word which arouses erotic and gastronomic memories among the skirted sex and memories gastronomic and erotic among the bearded sex."

Jean Anthelme Brillat-Savarin, the father of gastronomy (1755–1826)

musty, stinky wine

Red wines can often be described as having aromas of barnyard, wet soil, horse sweat and even manure. These aromas are cherished by many wine lovers. I would venture to say that the same gastronome who loves aged beef, truffles and very ripe brie enjoys reds possessing these musty, funky smells.

In some cases, such smells are believed to develop in wine when it's infected with a yeast known as "Brett." Brett is the nickname for *Brettanomyces*, a non-spore-forming genus of yeast in the *Saccharomycetaceae* family. The presence of Brett in wine is one of the most controversial wine issues of recent times. Some scientists, experts and winemakers believe that Brett can contribute interesting aromas, flavors and complexity when present in wine at low levels. Others claim it's a wine fault, can spoil wine and is therefore undesirable. These experts claim the yeast forms on grapes and develops in wine barrels and within bottling lines as a result of unsanitary conditions.

While some experts believe these musty, funky smells are due to the presence of Brett, others feel they're desirable aromas and flavors that derive from the region's terroir. Wineries within the wine regions of Bordeaux, the Rhône in France and the Hunter Valley in Australia have become known for producing wines with these intriguing characteristics. It's even regarded as a "house style."

Despite the controversy, many wine lovers revere the musty, stinky aromas of Brett-affected wines. I'm certainly one of them.

TEXTURE AND TEMPERATURE

The trigeminal nerve is responsible for detecting pain, heat, cold and burning sensations in our mouths. It helps us instinctively recognize these reactions as warning signs of a variety of potentially harmful stimuli. This nerve also allows us to experience the rewarding effects of chemosensory irritations in wine and food, such as bubbles in sparkling wine, heat in soup and coolness in ice cream.

Texture

While drinking and eating, we use our sense of taste and our sense of smell. But we also enjoy wine and food because of our sense of touch. We experience their textures inside our mouths. They can be hard, smooth, sticky, crisp, effervescent, etc. We think we love the taste of butter. But we actually like the creamy, oily mouthfeel of this product, accompanied by the buttery aromas it releases while inside our mouths. An avocado is considered an aphrodisiac, partly due to its smooth and sensual flesh. The same holds true for the slippery texture of a raw oyster.

Fattiness in food

Fattiness is both a texture and a flavor. If you close your eyes and pinch your nose, all liquid oils appear to be similar. Olive, canola, sesame and coconut oils and liquid butter are all just liquids with equally oily mouthfeels. But the moment you release your fingers from your nose, your brain, informing you of the specific product you're actually tasting, registers the individual smell. Fats are used in cooking to add texture and flavor, but some foods such as avocados, salmon and beef possess natural fattiness. As you'll discover in the chapter The Allure of Comfort, fatty foods are often comfort foods, ones that are highly addictive and sinful.

Fattiness in wine

The level of alcohol in a wine is called its "viscosity." Grapes grown in the warm climates of such countries as South Africa, Australia and Chile attain high sugar levels due to the intensity of heat and long sunshine hours. The greater the sugar in the grape, the higher the alcohol produced during fermentation and present in the resulting wine. The viscosity of a wine is experienced on our palate as "fattiness." The higher the alcohol in a wine, the fattier its mouthfeel. Glycerol is a sugar alcohol and a by-product formed during the fermentation process. It's colorless and odorless, but makes a wine creamier and heavier. Glycerol enhances the ripeness of fruit flavors, as well. It's difficult, however, to detect glycerol in wine as it takes a background role and fuses with other elements, such as alcohol and/or sweetness. Sweetness also provides a tactile sensation on our palate, known as "fatty" and "heavy" mouthfeel. Icewine possesses a great deal of sweetness (in balance with its sourness, of course) and so feels quite fatty. This is why icewine partners so well with the fatty texture and fabulous flavor of foie gras.

During the wine-making process, some wines also undergo a secondary fermentation called malolactic fermentation. This process converts some of the wine's harsh malic acid into a much softer lactic acid (as is found in milk). This can give the resulting wine a creamier, fatty mouthfeel. Malolactic fermentation can also produce a chemical called diacetyl in the wine, which is experienced on the palate as a buttery flavor.

Temperature

Temperature is an intrinsic element of taste. In a restaurant we judge a chef's and a sommelier's capabilities based on the temperature of our food and wine when they arrive at our table. We expect an appetizer such as a phyllo-wrapped brie to be crunchy on the outside (texture), as well as hot, melted and creamy on the inside (temperature). We also enjoy the cold sensation of a sorbet. The combining of both hot and cold sensations in our wine and food experience can certainly contribute to a culinary orgasm. Hot crab cakes served alongside a chilled glass of bubbling champagne with yeasty aromas creates diametrical harmony.

Palatability

"The whole process of flavor perception is multi-sensory. We all have our own perception of life. Not only do we see, hear and taste differently but we have our own, individual personal experiences, emotion and memory. As long as this continues, the world of eating will be a very exciting place."

Heston Blumenthal, chef-owner of The Fat Duck in London, England

When a wine and food partnership tastes sublime, all our senses—taste, smell, touch, sight and hearing—are heightened. We experience spine-tingling ecstasy and a desire to moan with delight.

Through their senses, babies are equipped with the survival mechanisms their new world demands. In adulthood we continue to use these sensory systems, even when it comes to sipping wine and eating. Even so, we generally pay no attention to how they work together to formulate our culinary experiences. When we have a disappointing meal, often our immediate response is to blame external forces, such as the chef's or winemaker's lack of skill. While fresh ingredients, accomplished cooking techniques and expert wine-making abilities certainly play crucial roles in our dining, so, too, do our five senses.

One way to contribute to a moan-worthy culinary experience is to purposefully consider and create an environment that stimulates the five senses.

EAT WITH YOUR EYES

"The chemical senses, i.e., taste, smell and sensory irritation, are often considered to be the gatekeepers of the body, whose function is to detect what would be bad for the body and that should be rejected and to identify what the body needs for survival and that therefore should be consumed. Appearance is the primary cue of expectation and texture has practical concerns for palatability and preferences and both also play a role in flavor perception."

Sensory Science Research, University of Otago, New Zealand

When we're born, our sight is actually our least developed sense. As infants, we're "legally blind," although we do have the ability to distinguish the contrast between light and dark. Our vision develops rapidly throughout our early childhood.

Our sense of sight is also the first system we use in our perception of wine and food. Color is an important factor in both, as color is light and light is energy. Scientists have discovered that we experience physiological changes when we're exposed to certain colors. Colors stimulate, excite, depress, tranquilize, create a feeling of warmth or coolness and even increase our appetites.

The deep ruby shade of a glass of Pinot Noir in a Riedel wine glass sitting against an elegant white tablecloth is enough to entice any true wine lover to indulge. The rich red of a cooked lobster shell acting as the garnish on a platter of mini grilled lobster sandwiches makes us salivate. That's because our sense of sight helps stimulate our salivary glands. The appearance of food can cause the tiny muscles distributed throughout the salivary glands to contract, squeezing the watery contents from each gland. This may sound dull and scientific. However, the sight of a tray of colorful appetizers can certainly tantalize you and make you "drool." All great chefs know that presentation is essential to the desirability of a dish.

Visual Stimulus of Wine

The shape of a wine glass also lures the eye and the palate. In fact, the shape of a glass actually affects how we feel about the wine experience to come. An inexpensive, poorly shaped glass tells us that our experience will be mediocre and average, like the glass itself. But a well-shaped, quality glass suggests sophistication and inspires excitement and curiosity about the wine to be tasted.

Just as importantly, the shape of the glass plays a vital role in helping us detect the intensity of a wine's aromas. The way in which it makes the wine flow over the palate emphasizes certain tastes and flavors. One glass may bring out a wine's fruity aromas while another will stifle them. A properly shaped glass can highlight a wine's tanginess and make it taste refreshing. Yet a poorly shaped one can make this same taste sensation in the same wine seem harsh and metallic.

Look for glasses with a rim that's narrower than the bowl. This helps concentrate the aromas. A narrow rim also enhances flavors. A wide-rimmed glass requires us to bend our head forward to reach the wine without spilling it. In turn, this keeps the wine in the front of the inside of our mouth. A narrower rim, on the other hand, forces us to tilt our head backward. This allows the wine to flow over the tongue, thereby touching various taste zones, such as sour, sweet, bitter, etc. There is much controversy over whether a specifically shaped glass will actually deliver wine to a certain area of the tongue to highlight a particular taste sensation. The reason is that new scientific evidence suggests that our palates and the location of our taste buds are individualistic.

The color of a wine can also cause us to salivate. Red, which has long been considered dominant and dynamic, has an exciting and stimulating effect on us. Red wine even *looks* romantic; its intense color reminds us of passion. That's why red hearts on Valentine's Day spell romance and love. When entertaining, consider the color of your wine in relationship to your tablecloth, napkins and platters, as well as the colors of your appetizers.

THE SENSUOUS SOUND OF WINE AND FOOD

At birth, infants have a well-developed sense of hearing. In fact, recent research suggests that babies, while in utero, are already hearing sounds from the outside world. By the time they emerge, they already prefer the sound of their own mother's voice.

To a grown-up wine enthusiast, nothing is more appealing than the sound of wine flowing from a bottle into a decanter or glass. Sounds like that stir the appetite. The crunch of a tortilla chip, the sound of sizzling meat or the slurping of hot soup contribute to and heighten our dining experience. Tableside sounds are enticing, whether they're as festive as the soft pop of a cork bursting off a bottle of bubbly, or as routine as the sound of teeth contentedly chewing.

So when you're setting the stage for a romantic encounter or evening event, think about how sound can enhance your guests' enjoyment of the wine and your matching appetizers.

Consider, for instance, the music you play during your intimate rendezvous or event. I conduct workshops for corporations and organizations called Harmony on the Palate (based on my last book), Journey of the Senses© and the MOAN FACTOR. In my Journey of the Senses workshop, I blindfold participants. In one exercise, using a CD player, I play the song "Ave Maria," sung by the operatic pop vocal group Il Divo. The workshop participants are asked to relax and experience how the song affects the taste of a particular wine, usually a red. While the participants are still blindfolded and holding onto the same wine, I then switch to a new song, Electric Light Orchestra's hit "Turn to Stone." Their task? To smell and taste the same wine again. After the exercise I ask the participants to share with the group their personal experience of the tastes and flavors of the same wine while listening to different songs. The feedback is the same in every workshop. The group is generally split in its perceptions. Many participants say that, during "Ave Maria," the wine tastes soft and creamy and during "Turn to Stone," the wine tastes harsh and bitter. The rest of the group experiences the opposite.

I believe the participants' assessments result from the kinds of tasters they are. There is no "right" way to experience the wine. The point of the exercise is to show the power that our sense of sound has on our dining experience. The exercise reveals that our sense of sound alters how we perceive wine and food on our palate.

When entertaining a romantic partner or a large group, use music to aid in heightening your guests' experiences. And don't be shy about verbally sharing with your guests the event's menu and the tastes and flavors they're about to experience. Some restaurateurs understand the power of sound in the dining experience and so make sure the servers explain the intricate details of each dish. They recite the menu as though it's poetry. The reciting of a menu creates anticipation and stirs the appetite, thus helping to prepare your guests for their culinary orgasm.

TOUCHA, TOUCHA, TOUCHA, TOUCH ME!

Touch is an important sense that plays a crucial role in the cognitive development, sociability and immunological development of a child as well as in its ability to withstand stress. Infants are born with a relatively well-developed sense of touch.

This sophisticated sense of touch stays with us into adulthood. It's especially important for chefs and home cooks. We must use our fingers to feel the doneness of the filet mignon and know how much longer it needs to cook to reach the desired temperature. We touch food to distinguish temperature, moisture content and textures, as well.

Our sense of touch can also heighten our eating experience and contribute toward a culinary orgasm. It's quite appropriate to forgo a fork and use your hands to munch on appetizers. Any sex coach will tell you that eating with your hands is intimate and sensual. And let's not forget that feeding your romantic partner can be deliciously arousing.

The texture or feel of foods in our mouth can be orgasmic. Some foods have been designated as aphrodisiacs because of how they feel in our mouths. Fresh figs, for example, possess a sensual, creamy consistency and heady sweetness. They've also been inextricably tied to fertility and reproduction.

I often suggest that people be discriminating when picking their wine glasses. Before purchasing glasses, touch them. Feel the weight of the glass and texture of the stem. The feel of the wine glass in our hand and on our lips influences our perception and level of enjoyment of a wine and therefore our overall dining experience.

Our sense of touch also affects our perception of the taste and flavor of wine. In the same Journey of the Senses workshop mentioned above, I pour new wine into the participants' glasses. They're asked to smell and taste the wine, assessing its aromas, flavors and texture. I then ask them to touch a piece of synthetic poodle fabric, which is as soft and snuggly as the hair of a real poodle. Their next task is to sip the same wine while touching coarse sandpaper. Once again, the group is mostly divided. Some participants say the wine tastes rough when touching the poodle fabric and creamy while touching the sandpaper. The other participants experience the opposite reaction. To them, while touching the soft material, the wine tastes creamy. When they touch the sandpaper, the wine becomes bitter and sharp. Our sense of touch influences our perception of the flavor of wine and food. The feel of a quality cloth napkin flowing through our fingers provides us with a different perception than if we were to use a paper napkin against our flesh and lips.

So when planning a romantic evening or entertaining a group of friends, strategically create the sights, sounds and textures that will stimulate your guests' senses.

the *Allure* of comfort

You may be surprised at how mini versions of comfort foods are often the first appetizers devoured by guests. A grilled cheese sandwich is always scrumptious, whether it's presented in a full-sized portion or as a tiny bite. I don't know about you, but I lose self-control when given the opportunity to indulge in garlic mashed potatoes, even if they're just piped onto a canapé. Such comfort foods are addictive and satisfying. They cause us to moan in pure delight. They're also inexpensive, simple and easy to prepare. That's why they also make for great appetizers.

We all have our own idea of what constitutes a comfort food. Your preferences will be based on the kind of taster you are, as well as the culinary culture in which you grew up. One of the reasons comfort foods give us comfort is that they allow us to recall and celebrate our childhoods. As is generally the case, my comfort foods are the dishes that my mom and dad cooked and fed to my siblings and me when we were young. When I make these dishes today, even as bite-sized morsels, they evoke fond memories.

Besides inspiring nostalgia, comfort foods tend to be high in countless combinations of fat, salt, sweetness and umami—sensations that satisfy our palate. They can be high-protein foods or complex carbohydrates. Carbohydrates and fats increase the levels of two mood-boosting chemicals, serotonin and endorphins, in our brains. So comfort foods can also make us feel good.

I sometimes see recipes for "healthy" comfort foods. To me, that's as absurd as the concept of alcohol-free wine! Comfort foods give us comfort because they're an indulgence, satisfying our cravings and even our addictions. We experience satisfaction in knowing our physiological needs have been met—we're able to survive! When our needs are met—at least in that moment—we feel comforted.

Wine is also considered by many to be a comfort food. Some wines are downright orgasmic. In addition, the alcohol in wine alters brain chemistry. A glass of red after a stressful day acts as a natural tranquilizer, reducing anxiety and tension and creating a sense of comfort.

Truffle Mashed Potatoes with Garlic & Caramelized Leeks (page 182) served on Chinese soup spoons is an orgasmic version of the age-old comfort food, good ol' mashed potatoes. There are literally hundreds of old-fashioned yet delicious comfort foods from around the world that can be recreated as upscale appetizers.

The next time you're entertaining, consider creating a mini-sized version of your favorite comfort food. Besides being orgasmic, its fat and carbohydrates will also absorb alcohol, an extra favor to your guests.

This chart offers a few options from my list of comfort food favorites.

old-time comfort food	upscale appeal	matching wine
brownies	one-bite brownies using 86% cocoa or higher	tawny port
chicken pot pie	mini chicken pot pies in mini muffin tins	light, fruity red
chili con carne	chili con carne served in small cappuccino cups with stir spoons (keep the heat and spice gentle)	red with forward fruit
clam chowder	mini clam chowder served in shot glasses	big, fat white
corn dog	lobster dog	big, fat white
corn on the cob	bite-sized corn on the cob with lemon and thyme (fresh lemon juice, sea salt and finely chopped fresh thyme)	crisp, light white
french fries	french fries tossed in hot pesto and served in mini newspaper cones	big, fat white
fried chicken	mini deep-fried drumlets	big, fat white
grilled cheese	grilled cheese using sourdough bread, extra-old cheddar cheese and freshly grated black pepper; butter outside, sprinkle with Asiago and fry in bacon fat	big, fat white or red with forward fruit
macaroni and cheese	macaroni with white wine, Parmesan, Romano, fontina and truffle oil in small ramekins	big, fat white
mashed potatoes	truffled mashed potatoes with garlic, brie and bacon	austere red
meatloaf	bite-sized meatloaves	red with forward fruit
peanut butter and jelly sandwich	mini hazelnut butter (unsweetened) and raspberry preserve (use diabetic so it's not too sweet to pair with wine)	off-dry rosé
pizza	pizzettas with wild mushrooms, Gorgonzola and bacon	austere red
potato salad	bite-sized portions of lobster potato salad	big, fat white
potato skins	mini potato skins with brie and bacon	big, fat chardonnay
shepherd's pie	bite-sized shepherd's pies with diced lamb and root vegetables and garlic mashed potato topping (baked in small ramekins)	austere red
spaghetti	slices of baked spaghetti pie	light, fruity red or red with forward fruit
tourtière	mini tourtières served in ramekins	light, fruity red

tantric twosomes & titillating trios

The key to homemade appetizers with the MOAN FACTOR lies in finding ingredient combinations that naturally harmonize. These magical flavor combinations are integral to creating sublime tastes, flavors and textures.

Sensory scientists still don't have a complete understanding of why certain ingredient combinations are so scrumptious. However, they do know that one source of this heightening and persistence of flavor comes from synergistic umami combined with other ingredients. Tomatoes (basic umami) paired with Parmigiano-Reggiano (synergistic umami) and basil are a great example of an orgasmic medley of three.

But using umami is not the only way for a food partnership to get the MOAN FACTOR. There are other ingredient combinations that don't necessarily create umami, but are considered great partners, like olive oil and garlic or apples and cinnamon. The source of their harmony remains a mystery, but great chefs keep these combinations in their repertoires.

Here is a small list of the thousands of orgasmic flavor combinations you can use to spice up your next appetizer soiree. One important factor in creating orgasmic combinations is using fresh ingredients. The following combinations refer to their fresh versions.

TANTRIC TWOSOMES

Apple and cheddar cheese

Apple and cinnamon

Apple and fennel

Arugula and feta

Avocado and cilantro

Avocado and lime

Avocado and lobster

Beef and black bean sauce

Brie and mango

Brie and pesto

Blue cheese and bacon

Capicolla and mozzarella

Carrots, orange and thyme

Carrots and mint

Cheddar cheese and beer

Cheddar cheese and broccoli

Cheddar cheese and mushrooms

Chicken and lemongrass

Chicken and pesto

Cream cheese and caviar

Dark chocolate and chili

Dark chocolate and mascarpone

Dark chocolate and Parmigiano-Reggiano

Dark chocolate and raspberry

Dark chocolate and walnuts

Garlic and ginger

Garlic and olive oil

Garlic and oregano

Garlic and rosemary

Goat cheese and cranberries

Goat cheese and fruit jellies

Goat cheese and pine nuts

Goat cheese and sun-dried tomatoes

Lamb and mint

Lemon and oregano

Lemon and potato

Lemon zest and pepper

Lime and shrimp

Mango and banana

Mango and lime

Melon and cardamom

Mushroom and bacon

Mushroom and prosciutto

Mushroom and rosemary

Orange zest and black peppercorns

Orange zest and chicken stock

Parsley and garlic

Parsley and grated lemon

Potatoes and sour cream

Prosciutto and asparagus

Prosciutto and cantaloupe

Prosciutto and figs

Prosciutto and melon

Prosciutto and Parmigiano-Reggiano

Rice and saffron

Smoked salmon and black peppercorns

Smoked salmon and capers

Smoked salmon and cream cheese

Smoked salmon and dill

Smoked salmon and lemon

Smoked salmon and Vidalia onion

Sour cream and chives

Strawberries and vanilla

Sun-dried tomatoes and goat cheese

Tomatoes and anchovy

Tomatoes and basil

Tomatoes and goat cheese

Truffles and olive oil

Tuna and capers

White balsamic vinegar and olive oil

TITILLATING TRIOS

Asparagus, Parmigiano-Reggiano and garlic

Beef, horseradish and sour cream

Beef, sun-dried tomatoes and black truffle oil

Beef, truffles and rosemary

Brie, bacon and potato

Brie, wild mushrooms and rosemary

Cheddar cheese, bacon and garlic

Chicken, apricot and brie

Chicken, brie and red pepper

Chicken, chives and parsley

Chicken, coconut and galangal

Chicken, goat cheese and pine nuts

Crème fraîche, lemon and horseradish

Dark chocolate, chilies and cardamom

Dark chocolate, rosemary and mint

Figs, balsamic vinegar and vanilla

Garlic, cilantro and ginger

Garlic, lemon and olive oil

Garlic, lemon and thyme

Goat cheese, prosciutto and figs

Goat cheese, whole black pepper-corns and olive oil

Lamb, brie and rosemary

Lamb, Dijon mustard and rosemary

Mango, toasted sesame seeds and chili oil

Olive oil, balsamic vinegar and Parmigiano-Reggiano

Olive oil, lemon juice and garlic

Onion, bacon and ham

Orange, red onion and mint

Orange and dark chocolate

Pear, Gorgonzola and toasted walnuts

Pork, apricot and brie

Pork tenderloin, applesauce and cranberries

Pork tenderloin, thyme and cumin

Potatoes, broccoli and cheddar cheese

Potatoes, sour cream and chives

Salmon, cedar and lemon

Shrimp, cilantro and lime

Smoked salmon, lemon and capers

Smoked salmon, lemon and dill

Soy, ginger and sesame oil

Sweet potatoes, curry and apple

Sweet potatoes, maple and balsamic

Sweet potatoes, maple and Jack Daniel's

Sweet potatoes, maple and smoked ham

Tomatoes, basil and olive oil

Tomatoes, bocconcini and balsamic vinegar

Tomatoes, bocconcini and olive oil

Tomatoes, goat cheese and olive oil

Venison, juniper berries and lemon

Venison, red currants and pomegranates

White chocolate, lavender and Earl Grey tea

AN ORGY OF FLAVORS

Chicken, coconut, lemongrass, galangal, garlic and lime

Chili, ginger, onion, garlic, coconut, cumin, coriander, cardamom, cinnamon, curry and turmeric

Ginger, garlic, tamarind, cumin, turmeric, coriander seeds and cayenne

Lemon, potatoes, olive oil and capers

Olive oil, garlic, tomatoes and basil

Soy sauce, coconut, chili pepper and ground peanuts

Soy sauce, sesame oil, fish sauce and rice vinegar

Szechuan pepper, chili, dried orange peel, poppy seeds, black sesame seeds, tamarind and seaweed

Thyme, rosemary, savory, oregano and lavender

White balsamic vinegar, olive oil and tomatoes

Mood & culture

While a party's mood and its prevailing culture might seem to be the least significant aspects of the culinary orgasm, they're actually the most important. They're the driving factor determining whether we ultimately accept a specific wine and food experience.

MOOD

Our mood alters our experience of almost everything that comes into our view and proximity. Unfortunately, when entertaining, we have no control over the moods of our guests, a factor that we must recognize and accept.

If you're in a depressed state, even the sight of a breathtaking table setting, the sound of lovely music or smells that would normally make your tummy growl in anticipation won't entice you. Your mood can also alter your experience of the taste of wine. When you're stressed, your gastrointestinal system is acidic, causing the palate to be acidic. An acidic palate will alter the taste of the acid in the wine. It can taste metallic, brassy and offensive. This is one reason the same wine can taste so different from one day to the next.

While we have no control over the moods of others, we can be cognizant of our own. Being unorganized and unprepared when hosting an event will cause you to be stressed. Your guests will immediately notice that you're anxious and detached and this will directly affect their level of comfort. More importantly, a stressful environment doesn't help your guests experience a culinary orgasm. That's why it's important to be organized and keep things simple. (Read the chapter The Art of Getting Organized.)

CULTURE

Your ethnicity plays a role in your ability to smell and taste flavors, as well as your enjoyment of certain ingredients. Research on genetics, race and taste are still being explored. However, science has shown how certain ethnic groups are able to detect specific tastes better than others. Asians, for example, are more likely to be super-tasters than are Caucasians.

Gear the cultural theme of your appetizers and wines to the taste preferences of the majority of your guests or to your romantic partner. Determine the kind of tasters they are and consider their ethnicity and taste preferences. I have one friend, a Canadian woman of Middle Eastern descent, who is a super-taster; she loves healthy North American dishes like a grilled tuna sandwich. She also enjoys Mediterranean and Middle Eastern flavors—like lemon, olive oil and garlic. The flavors of India, Thailand, China and Africa are of no interest to her. If she were one of my guests, I would be sure to include in my appetizer menu a few comfort foods like mini grilled cheese sliders and mini shepherd's pies. I might also create a few Middle Eastern appetizers, as well, such as foul mudammas on garlic toasts. (Foul mudammas is a Middle Eastern fava bean dip.)

The following chart shows the process of how we experience food, moving from our basic tastes to our environment, habituation, social situation and culture.

Food acceptability

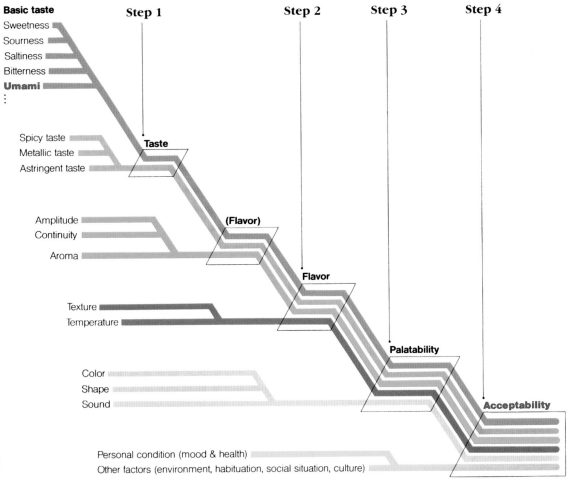

UMAMI INFORMATION CENTER, JAPAN

the Art of getting organized

There's mastery to home entertaining. A few guidelines will help you keep preparations simple. The more organized you feel, the better your mood! The better your mood, the greater your chance of creating an environment that supports your romantic partner or guests experiencing a culinary orgasm.

Here's a list of guidelines to aid your preparations.

THINK AHEAD

Always clean and shop the day before your event. This gives you time to decompress, make a few last-minute appetizers and focus on your own appearance.

TIME OF DAY AND DRESS CODE

What time of day would work best for your event? Do you plan on hosting a romantic get-together, a dinner party, a cocktail party or an evening bash? Is your event formal, semi-formal or casual? Be sure to mention these details on invitations so your guests can set aside the appropriate amount of time and dress accordingly. If you're planning a romantic interlude, these points are of less importance.

CLEAN OUT THE CLOSET

I've attended many events where my winter coat was thrown on the host's bed underneath a large pile of other coats. At the end of the evening it's annoying to have to hunt for my coat in order to leave. Clean out a closet so your guests can hang up their coats. This little detail creates a seamless beginning and ending to your event, affecting the mood of your guests as they arrive and as they leave.

THE SHOPPING LIST

Read through the recipes in their entirety while making the shopping list for your ingredients. (Always reserve an hour on preparation day to run out to obtain last-minute items.) The moment you arrive home, trim the stems of your fresh herbs. Stand them upright in a small bowl of water, cover it with a plastic bag and place it in the refrigerator. This will keep your herbs fresh for your recipes and garnishes.

THE MOOD

The mood you set arouses emotions and stimulates thought. Think about the mood you intend to create for your event. Lighting contributes significantly to ambience. Romantic evenings are best celebrated by candlelight, but large events can benefit from different lighting styles.

Lighting

Consider the lighting of the rooms in which your guests will be sitting or mingling. Do you want the atmosphere to be bright and happy, dim and comfortable, or interesting and dramatic? The area where your appetizers and wine are to be served should be well lit. This is so guests can see what they're eating and can read wine labels.

Music

As discussed in the chapter Palatability, the music you play at your party will not only make or break the mood of your event, but also affect the tastes and flavors of your appetizers and wine. So be sure to choose the appropriate music for the tone you want to set.

Scents

Refrain from using scents to create mood, as these smells will interfere with the aromas of your hot appetizers and wines. (This includes your wearing strong perfume, especially if you, personally, are serving the appetizers to guests.)

FLORAL DECOR

Fresh flowers help support the mood you intend to create. If using candlelight or low lighting, choose flowers in warm colors, such as orange, yellow and red. Cooler shades, such as blue and purple, don't suggest romance or intimacy. In brightly lit rooms, buy flowers in deeper hues, such as burgundy, deep blue and dark purple.

Since you're interested in causing a culinary orgasm for your guest(s), think about the details and cohesiveness of the entire event. The fresh flowers you choose, for instance, can echo the colors in the national flag of the country whose ethnic cuisine and wines you intend to serve. If you're focusing on Chinese cuisine, consider red and gold (yellow) flowers for good luck. If serving classic, European dishes, pastels create a traditional mood. Be sure to keep your fresh flowers away from fruit trays. Fruit puts off ethylene gas, which can cause some flowers to wilt.

INVITATIONS

Romantic dinners don't require a written invitation. However, if you're hosting a much larger party, send out invitations. The invitation itself should reflect the mood, dress code and theme of your gathering. Send out invitations from six to two weeks before the event.

HOW MUCH WINE AND FOOD TO SERVE

When considering how much food to serve with wine, think about the time of your event, where your guests will be coming from (work or home?) and where they may be headed afterward. Also take into consideration the other food you may be serving later, such as a main course or dessert.

Wine stimulates the appetite, so count on serving more appetizers than you might when people are drinking other beverages.

Luncheons

Before luncheons your guests will eat few appetizers. Serve two appetizers and expect guests to enjoy one to two pieces of each. Offer one wine style, serving a 2-ounce (50 mL) portion to accompany two harmonizing appetizers.

Dinner Party

If you're hosting a dinner party over the course of an entire evening, count on making four appetizers, with each guest enjoying about four of each. Serve two wine styles and offer two harmonizing appetizers for each style. Again, serve no more than 2-ounce (50 mL) portions of wine with each tidbit. Your guests will also drink wine during dinner.

Cocktail Event

If you're hosting a cocktail event, plan on making six to eight different appetizers and count on guests devouring about 10 to 12 pieces each. A good rule is to prepare more than you think you'll need. Keep a few baskets of baguettes and specialty cheeses on hand. Since wine will be served, make sure to include appetizers that are high in fat and carbohydrates to absorb the alcohol.

Create stations

Create wine and appetizer stations. Each station can pair one wine style with two appetizers. Use clean glasses at each station. Or provide a jug of water and a spittoon at each station. This is so guests can swish their glasses with water to remove the remainder of one wine before pouring another. Plan on one bottle of wine providing about 10 portions (2 ounces/50 mL) each.

Glasses

The shape of the glass plays a role in our enjoyment of wine. (See the section called Visual Stimulus of Wine on page 30.) Give some thought to the quality of your glasses and to serving each wine in a glass that will enhance an appreciation of its individual characteristics.

PRESENTATION

We eat with our eyes. When it comes to creating appetizers with the MOAN FACTOR, consider their presentation.

The Serving Table

You'll have to decide in advance if you'll hire serving staff or present your appetizers yourself on a table. Obviously the latter choice is the least expensive.

- Choose a white tablecloth and white linen if your platters offer a variety of colors. If your dishware is plain white, use a colorful tablecloth and matching linen scheme.

- Create a centerpiece for the table. The centerpiece can be made from fruits, vegetables or flowers.

- Choose differently shaped and textured breads, served in a variety of baskets. Leave some whole and slice the others.

Platters

- Use differently shaped and colored platters.

- Decorate the platters with garnishes before adding appetizers.

- Spread the appetizers out, so they're not piled up.

- Use other containers and surfaces to serve as platters, such as bowls, baskets, cutting boards, wooden planks, flower pots and saucers, martini glasses, cappuccino cups and saucers, shot glasses, Chinese soup spoons and even ceramic floor tiles. Sterilize these items in advance.

- Consider creating a traditional and elegant atmosphere by serving appetizers and the main entrée on white serving platters and plates.

- Create a theme for the presentation. If serving Chinese cuisine, serve appetizers on bamboo mats over a cutting board or in a metal wok or a bamboo steamer.

- Offer no more than two different appetizers on each platter.

Garnishes

If appetizers offer plenty of color, they'll need little garnishing. Be creative. Garnishes can include edible flowers, banana leaves, grape leaves, fresh herbs and even linen napkins. Linen helps soak up grease more effectively than paper napkins and towels. Linen also feels better to the touch, affecting how the wine and appetizers taste. (See Palatability on page 29.)

- Keep garnishes fresh, local and small so they don't overshadow the appetizers.

- Choose garnishes that reflect the ingredients in the appetizer recipes. If serving an artichoke and Parmigiano-Reggiano dip, for example, artichoke hearts and Parmesan shavings can work nicely as garnishes.

- Fresh herbs such as thyme, rosemary, chives and Italian parsley make attractive garnishes. Basil and cilantro droop. Dill is too aromatic and will overshadow other primary aromas.

- If serving fried foods, forgo greens and lettuce as a garnish because they'll wilt.

Appetizers

- Use fresh, local ingredients and make bite-sized pieces, uniform in their dimensions and shape.
- Refrain from repeating flavors, if possible.
- Pick recipes that can be assembled at different times. In other words, don't choose appetizers that all need to be prepared as guests are arriving. Pick some that can be made the day before and on the morning of the event.
- Appetizers should reflect the guests' preferences. Some events, such as family gatherings, may benefit from simple comfort food appetizers, while other events call for a more sophisticated menu.
- Recipes should celebrate foods in season and the occasion itself, such as creating dishes with tomatoes in the summer and sweet potatoes for a holiday dinner in the winter.
- Think about how the appetizers will be served—on small plates or on napkins? With forks or without? The recipes you choose should suit the serving style.
- Consider the shapes and colors of the appetizers. Refrain from putting foods of the same color on the same plate.
- Vary the texture of dips. If one is smooth and velvety, contrast it with another in a chunkier style.
- Serve appetizers at different temperatures—chilled, room temperature and warm. Offer variety, from rich and fatty to light and low fat. Some morsels can be fancy, others, simple and elegant. Serve the chilled and

room-temperature bites first to match the wines to be served—whites before reds, chilled wines before room-temperature ones.

- Wait until guests have sampled the chilled wines and room-temperature appetizers before heating the rest. The smell of hot appetizers, while pleasing, will interfere with the aromas and textures of the others.
- If you're serving appetizers at stations, set up a tent card explaining why each one works with its accompanying wine. (You can copy the information directly from the wine notes in each recipe of Part Two.)
- When you're hosting a romantic evening, refrain from appetizers highlighting garlic and raw onions. Fresh breath is important.

Here's a list summing up the primary details you need to determine and organize before your event. Once you've handled these, you'll be ready to create wine and food pairings with the MOAN FACTOR.

Number of guests	Wine shopping list
Theme	Shopping list for garnishes
Time of day	Lighting in room
Dress code	Music
Invitations to be created by a specific date	Flowers
Invitations to be sent by a specific date	Tablecloths and other linens
Booking serving staff	Serving platters
Scheduling invitation follow-up calls	Individual serving plates or napkins?
Cleaning out closet for coats	Cutlery, if needed
Creating menu and matching wines (include at least two umami-rich appetizers)	Wine glasses
	Ice buckets to chill white wines
	Water jugs and spittoons
Appetizer shopping list	Scheduling time for heating hot appetizers

2

orgasmic appetizers to *pair* with...

Sparkling wines

PREDOMINANT BUILDING BLOCKS

Sourness and fruitiness in dry sparkling wines.

Sourness, fruitiness and some sweetness in off-dry sparkling wines.

FLAVORS

From lemon, peach and tropical to complex, yeasty, toasty and woody.

WINES PRODUCED IN THE SPARKLING STYLE

- Sparkling wines that have undergone barrel fermentation or aging tend to offer creamy texture with vanilla, toasty, yeasty and spicy flavors.

- Sparkling wines can be light-, medium- or full-bodied.

- Three main grape varieties are used to produce champagne and sparkling wines. They are Pinot Noir, Pinot Meunier and Chardonnay.

- Top-quality sparkling wines and champagne are made in the classic French process called *méthode champenoise*, which gives them complexity and tiny, long-lasting bubbles.

- Best food matches depend upon whether the wine is bone-dry (brut) or offers sweetness. Brut versions work nicely with salty ingredients, such as raw oysters, caviar, goat cheese, feta and smoked salmon.

- Off-dry versions go nicely with fresh fruit and cold fruit soups, fatty cheeses, fruit preserves and hot and spicy appetizers and entrées.

The regions at right are noted for producing sparkling wines and champagne.

REGIONS

champagne
France (Champagne)

others
Australia
Austria
Canada (British Columbia, Ontario)
France
Germany
Italy
New Zealand
Spain
United States (California, Oregon, Washington State)

orgasmic south american shooter

This is a highly textured "shooter," offering layers of taste and flavor. The sparkling wine will clean and prepare your palate for the next culinary adventure. You can use any aged rum in this recipe, but I prefer to use Pampero Ron Anejo Selección 1938 rum.

*Serves 4–6
(makes 4–6 shooters)*

3		fresh lime wedges
½ cup	125 mL	demerara brown sugar
½ cup	125 mL	freshly ground coffee
6 oz	175 mL	aged rum
4–6		shooter glasses

Cut the limes into 4 wedges each. Place the lime wedges, sugar and coffee in separate bowls. As guests arrive, have them take a wedge of fresh lime, dipping 1 side in sugar. Dip the other side in freshly ground coffee. Take a small bite of the lime, getting some of the juice, sugar and coffee into your mouth. While the juice, sugar and coffee are still in your mouth, take a sip of the rum and let the flavors mingle.

building blocks
The predominant building blocks are sourness from the lime, sweetness from the sugar and bitterness from the coffee. Choose an off-dry sparkling wine to pair with the sweetness left in your mouth from this shooter.

flavors
Choose an off-dry sparkling wine with citrus flavors to bring out the taste of lime left in your mouth.

blackened oysters

		all-purpose flour (for dredging)
2		eggs, beaten with 2 Tbsp (25 mL) milk
¼ cup	50 mL	Orgasmic Culinary Creations Cajun Quickie dry rub*
½ cup	125 mL	dried breadcrumbs
¼ cup	50 mL	cornmeal
¼ cup	50 mL	peanut oil (for frying)
18		fresh oysters, shucked
¼ cup	50 mL	butter
		sour cream (as needed)

*Turn to the last page for more details on how to purchase Cajun Quickie. You can also season these oysters with homemade Creole Seasoning (see page 218).

Pour the flour for dredging into a bowl. Combine the beaten eggs and milk in another bowl. Combine the Cajun Quickie, breadcrumbs and cornmeal in a third bowl.

Heat the peanut oil in a skillet over medium heat. Dredge the oysters in flour, dip them in the egg mixture and roll them in the bread-crumbs. Add the oysters and 1 Tbsp (15 mL) of the butter to the hot oil. Fry the oysters until they're golden brown on all sides, about 2 minutes.

Drain them on paper towels. Repeat for all the oysters. Place 1 blackened oyster in a Chinese soup spoon. Add a dollop of sour cream to each spoon.

building blocks
The predominant building block is heat and spice from the Cajun Quickie. An off-dry sparkling wine has enough sweetness to offset it.

flavors
Choose an off-dry sparkling wine with some yeasty and creamy tones to match the sour cream topping.

smoked salmon spread

This is a simple spread that allows the flavors of the smoked salmon to shine through. Look for a cold-smoked version. Cold smoking takes hours or even days. The smoke wafts past the salmon, which is situated in a separate area from the actual fire. No direct cooking takes place, so the interior of the salmon remains moist.

Serves 4–6

8 oz	250 g	cream cheese
2 Tbsp	25 mL	sour cream
1 tsp	5 mL	freshly squeezed lemon juice
1		small red onion, diced
2 tsp	10 mL	Worcestershire sauce
6 oz	175 g	smoked salmon, broken into chunks
2 Tbsp	25 mL	finely chopped fresh dill
		flatbread

Combine the cream cheese, sour cream, lemon juice, onion and Worcestershire sauce in a bowl and mix them together with a fork until smooth. Carefully fold in the salmon pieces and the dill. Transfer the mixture to a serving bowl. Cover it and chill it for 30 minutes. Serve it with flatbread.

building blocks
The predominant building blocks are sourness from the lemon and saltiness from the smoked salmon. A brut sparkling wine has enough sourness to harmonize with the lemon and offset the saltiness.

flavors
Choose a brut sparkling wine with citrus flavors to match the lemon flavor of this spread.

addictive chinese pork dumplings

You'll need at least 50 of these little fellas to satisfy four to six people as they're highly addictive. Dumpling wrappers are available at Asian supermarkets.

Serves 4–6 (makes 50 dumplings)

Umami-rich dipping sauce:

½ cup	125 mL	light Chinese soy sauce
2 Tbsp	25 mL	rice vinegar
1 Tbsp	15 mL	sesame oil
1 Tbsp	15 mL	minced fresh ginger
1		green onion, finely chopped

Dumplings:

1½ cups	375 mL	finely chopped Chinese cabbage
1 tsp	5 mL	salt
1 lb	500 g	minced pork
15		garlic chives, finely chopped
2 Tbsp	25 mL	light Chinese soy sauce
1 Tbsp	15 mL	rice vinegar
2 Tbsp	25 mL	sesame oil
1 Tbsp	15 mL	minced fresh ginger
1 Tbsp	15 mL	cornstarch
50		round dumpling wrappers
		cornstarch (as needed)
		water (as needed)
		corn oil (for frying)

For the sauce, combine the soy sauce, vinegar and sesame oil in a bowl. Mix well. Stir in the fresh ginger and the green onion. Cover the bowl and refrigerate the dipping sauce until it's needed, up to 8 hours.

To make the filling, mix the cabbage with the salt in a bowl and let the mixture sit for 30 minutes. Squeeze the excess water from the cabbage. Add the pork, chives, soy sauce, rice vinegar, sesame oil, ginger and cornstarch. Mix them together well. Drain off any excess liquid.

Place a dumpling wrapper on a clean work surface. Place 1 tsp (5 mL) of filling in the center of the wrapper. Spread a little water along the edges of the wrapper, using your finger. Fold the wrapper in half, making a half-moon. Using your thumb and index finger, form pleats along the sealed edges. Repeat until all the wrappers are used. Place the completed dumplings on a baking tray sprinkled with cornstarch.

Fill a skillet with water. Bring the water to a boil over high heat. Add half the dumplings. Stir them so they don't stick together. Cook the dumplings for 8 or 9 minutes, or until the pork is cooked. Set the steamed dumplings on a plate coated with a little oil. Repeat until all the dumplings are made.

Heat corn oil in a skillet over medium heat. Fry the dumplings, tossing them frequently, until they're golden. Serve them warm with the dipping sauce.

building blocks
The predominant building block is saltiness from the soy sauce. A crisp, brut sparkling wine has sourness to offset the salt.

flavors
Choose a brut sparkling wine with yeasty flavors to complement the doughy flavor of the dumpling skins.

virgin cherries stuffed with goat cheese

One of my favorite local food shops in East City, Peterborough, is called Firehouse Gourmet. That's where I picked up a bottle of extra virgin olive oil infused with white truffles, an expensive French oil produced by Duo. It's well worth its price. Using this olive oil as a finishing ingredient, I served my husband a few of these little tomatoes before dinner. When he asked for more tomatoes instead of dinner, I knew these babies were worthy of this book.

Serves 4–6 (makes 24 stuffed tomatoes)

24		large cherry tomatoes (washed and dried)
4 oz	125 g	fresh goat cheese
		sea salt to taste
		freshly ground black pepper to taste
		white truffle olive oil or extra virgin olive oil
24		tiny basil tops or oregano leaves (for garnish)

Carefully cut a small portion off the bottom of each tomato so that it sits flat.

Slice off a thin portion from the top of each tomato. Using a melon baller, scoop out the flesh, being careful not to break the skin. Discard the flesh. To make the filling, combine the goat cheese, salt and pepper in a medium bowl. Mix them together with a fork until the mixture is smooth. Fill each tomato shell with 1 tsp (5 mL) of the goat cheese mixture. Set a basil top or 3 tiny oregano leaves in the center of each tomato. Drizzle each tomato with truffle olive oil. Set the tomatoes on a plate. Cover and chill until you're ready to serve them.

building blocks
The predominant building block is sourness from the fresh tomatoes and goat cheese. A brut sparkling wine with sourness is a tasty match.

flavors
Choose a brut sparkling wine with some lemon flavor to match the sourness of the appetizer.

caviar lovers' dip

This is a quick and easy dip for those who crave caviar with sparkling wine! It's the ideal treat for you and your romantic partner. If you like, you can substitute lumpfish for the caviar.

Serves 4–6

6 oz	175 g	whipped cream cheese
3 oz	90 g	sour cream
1 Tbsp	25 mL	freshly squeezed lemon juice
½		red onion, finely diced
2 oz	60 g	fresh caviar (preferably black)
2 Tbsp	25 mL	finely chopped fresh dill
		freshly ground black pepper to taste
		flatbread

Combine the cream cheese and sour cream in a bowl. Fold in the lemon juice and red onion. Carefully fold in the caviar and dill. Season with pepper. Cover and refrigerate the dip until needed, but no longer than 4 hours. Serve with flatbread.

building blocks
The predominant building blocks are sourness from the cream cheese and sour cream and saltiness from the caviar. A brut sparkling wine is sour enough to match the base of this dip, while nicely offsetting its saltiness.

flavors
Choose a brut sparkling wine with citrus notes to complement the flavor of the caviar.

white bean & parmesan toasts

*Look closely at the
Parmigiano-Reggiano
in this dish. You'll see
that it contains small
crystals—glutamate
crystals formed during
the aging process,
making this cheese high
in synergistic umami.*

*Serves 4–6
(makes 12 toasts)*

1 cup	250 mL	cooked white beans
¾ cup	175 mL	freshly grated Parmigiano-Reggiano
1 tsp	5 mL	freshly squeezed lemon juice
1 cup	250 mL	olive oil
2 Tbsp	25 mL	finely chopped fresh basil
		sea salt to taste
		freshly ground black pepper to taste
6		slices whole wheat bread
¼ cup+	50 mL+	corn oil (for frying)

Combine the white beans, Parmigiano and lemon juice in a food
processor or blender. Pulsate the mixture until it's blended. Slowly
add the olive oil in a steady stream and purée the mixture until it's
creamy. Transfer it to a bowl. Fold in the basil. Season the spread
with salt and pepper. Cover it and keep it at room temperature, for no
more than 2 hours, until it's needed.

Roll out a slice of bread using a rolling pin. Cut out 2 circles that are
2 inches (5 cm) in diameter, using the rim of a wine glass or a cookie
cutter. Repeat for the remaining slices. You should have 12 circles.

Add ¼ cup (50 mL) oil to a skillet. Heat the oil until it's hot but not
smoking. Fry the slices of bread for about 30 seconds per side until
they're golden. You'll need to add more oil. Remove the toasts from
the skillet and drain them on paper towel. Spread about 2 Tbsp
(25 mL) of the white bean mixture onto each toast. Serve the toasts
at room temperature.

building blocks
The predominant building blocks are sourness from the lemon
and saltiness from the Parmigiano. A brut sparkling wine has
enough sourness to match and nicely offsets the saltiness.

flavors
Choose a brut sparkling wine with citrus notes to complement the
lemon flavor.

southwest tequila & lime marinated shrimp

Tequila and lime is a Southwestern flavor combination. It's one of those mysterious partnerships that will make you moan despite the fact that these ingredients aren't high in fat, carbohydrates, salt or umami.

Serves 4–6 (makes 18 shrimp)

18		large shrimp, peeled and deveined
18		lime wedges
½ cup	125 mL	freshly squeezed lime juice
1 tsp	5 mL	lime zest
1 cup	250 mL	tequila
3		cloves garlic, minced
2		medium shallots, finely chopped
2 tsp	10 mL	roasted cumin seeds
		sea salt to taste
		freshly ground black pepper to taste
½ cup	125 mL	vegetable oil
¼ cup	50 mL	finely chopped cilantro
2 tsp	10 mL	lime juice
6		bamboo skewers (6 inch/15 cm), soaked overnight in water (soak some extras just in case; they're cheap)

Thread 1 shrimp, then 1 lime wedge on a skewer. Repeat 2 more times, so each skewer holds 3 shrimp and 3 lime wedges. Repeat for all 6 skewers. Lay the skewers in a shallow glass dish large enough to hold them, in 1 layer if possible.

To make the marinade, combine the lime juice, zest, tequila, garlic, shallots, cumin, salt and pepper in a bowl. (To roast the cumin seeds, place them in a dry skillet over medium heat and cook for about 2 minutes, until they become aromatic.) Slowly add the oil, whisking the mixture until it's combined. Taste it for seasoning. Pour the marinade over the shrimp. Cover and refrigerate the skewers for 45 minutes.

Prepare the barbecue for medium-heat grilling. Grill the shrimp skewers for about 6 minutes, 3 minutes per side or until the shrimp are cooked. Remove them from the grill. Sprinkle them with the cilantro and lime juice. Serve the skewers warm or at room temperature. The limes can be sliced and their flesh eaten.

building blocks
The predominant building block is sourness from the lime juice. A brut sparkling wine has enough sourness to match.

flavors
Choose a sparkling wine with citrus notes to harmonize with the flavor of lime.

sweet island satays

My good friend Chef David Franklin developed this recipe to celebrate my Sweet Jerk artisan dry rub for wine lovers.

Serves 4–6 (makes 16 satays)

2		chicken breasts, about 6 oz (175 g) each
1 Tbsp	15 mL	freshly squeezed lime juice
2 Tbsp	25 mL	dark rum
1 Tbsp	15 mL	minced shallots
2 Tbsp	25 mL	Orgasmic Culinary Creations Sweet Jerk dry rub*
8		slices prosciutto, cut in half lengthwise
16		bamboo skewers (6 inch/15 cm), soaked overnight in water (soak some extras just in case; they're cheap)

*Turn to the last page for more details on how to purchase Sweet Jerk. You can substitute with homemade Jamaican Seasoning (see page 219).

Cut the chicken breasts into sixteen ½-inch (1 cm) strips. Place the strips in a nonreactive bowl and mix them with the lime juice, rum, shallots and Sweet Jerk. Cover the chicken and refrigerate it for at least 2 hours.

Prepare the barbecue for medium-heat grilling. Wrap the chicken strips in the prosciutto and thread them onto the skewers.

Sear the wrapped chicken skewers over high heat for about 1½ minutes per side and then move them to a cooler part of the grill until the center of the chicken is cooked through. Serve hot or at room temperature.

building blocks
The predominant building blocks are saltiness from the prosciutto and heat and spice from the Sweet Jerk. An off-dry sparkling wine has enough sourness to offset the prosciutto and enough sweetness to offset the heat and spice.

flavors
Choose a sparkling wine with lemon or lime flavors to harmonize with the fresh and tangy lime juice flavor imparted by the marinade.

baked greek feta with black olives & artichoke hearts

To offer a true traditional pairing, try a Greek brut sparkling wine. This appetizer can be prepared the night before your big event . . . or romantic escapade.

Serves 4–6

6		whole wheat pitas
1		piece Greek feta (8 oz/250 g)
¼ cup	50 mL	olive oil
4		kalamata olives pitted, sliced thinly
½ cup	125 mL	finely chopped marinated artichoke hearts
1 Tbsp	15 mL	finely chopped fresh oregano

Preheat the oven to 350°F (180°C). Separate the layers of each pita with a serrated knife. Stack 2 or 3 layers together and cut the pitas into quarters, or eighths, if you prefer. Spread the wedges out on 2 large baking sheets sprayed with nonstick cooking spray. Bake for about 20 minutes or until the pieces are golden. Cool them completely.

Place the feta on a large piece of foil. Drizzle the cheese with the olive oil. Top it with the olives and artichoke pieces. Sprinkle it with the oregano. Wrap the foil around the cheese and seal it. Place the foil-wrapped feta on a rimmed baking sheet. Bake it for 20 minutes or until the feta is hot. Using a large spoon, transfer the feta to a serving dish. Its consistency will resemble a dip. Serve it hot with pita crisps.

building blocks
The predominant building block is saltiness from the feta.
A brut sparkling wine has enough sourness to offset the saltiness.

flavors
Choose a brut sparkling wine with citrus notes to complement the flavor of the feta.

wanton shrimp (wontons) with marmalade dipping sauce

Use diabetic-friendly or sugar-reduced marmalade here. Regular marmalade is far too sweet to pair with any table wine.

Serves 4–6 (makes 36 wontons)

Filling:

6		cooked jumbo shrimp, tails removed, chopped
2		green onions, chopped
2		cloves garlic
1 Tbsp	15 mL	sesame oil
1 Tbsp	15 mL	rice vinegar
1 cup	250 mL	cream cheese
		sea salt and freshly ground black pepper to taste

Marmalade dipping sauce:

1 cup	250 mL	diabetic-friendly (or sugar-reduced) marmalade
¼ cup	50 mL	rice vinegar
½ tsp	2 mL	chili paste
36		wonton wrappers
		corn oil (for frying)

building blocks

The predominant building blocks are sweetness and heat and spice in the dipping sauce. Choose a sparkling wine with some sweetness to stand up to the sweet sauce and to offset the heat and spice.

flavors

Choose a sparkling wine with yeasty character to match the doughy flavor of the wonton skins.

For the filling, combine all the filling ingredients in a food processor or blender and purée the mixture until it forms a smooth paste. Season it with salt and pepper. Transfer it to a bowl, cover it and refrigerate it for an hour.

To make the dipping sauce, stir all the ingredients in a small bowl until well mixed. Cover and refrigerate until needed, but no longer than 4 hours.

Place several wonton skins on a dry, clean work surface. Brush the edges with water. Place ½ tsp (2 mL) of filling in the middle of each wonton skin. Fold the skin in half to form a triangle and seal.

Place about ¼ inch (5 mm) of oil in a large skillet. Heat it until the oil is sizzling. Pan-fry 6 wontons at a time in the skillet, until their edges turn up and are golden, about 30 seconds. Turn them quickly and fry the other side for 30 seconds. Remove the wontons and drain them on paper towel. Transfer the hot wontons to a serving platter and serve immediately with the dipping sauce.

shrimp & pork dumplings with umami thai dipping sauce

Fish sauce is loaded with umami, giving this dipping sauce depth of flavor. It's incredibly yummy.

Serves 4–6 (makes 30 dumplings)

Umami Thai dipping sauce:

½ cup	125 mL	Thai fish sauce
¾ cup	175 mL	freshly squeezed lime juice
2 Tbsp	25 mL	finely chopped fresh cilantro
2 Tbsp	25 mL	finely chopped fresh basil
2 Tbsp	25 mL	finely chopped fresh mint

Dumplings:

6 oz	175 g	raw shrimp, peeled and deveined
1 lb	500 g	minced pork
2 Tbsp	25 mL	Chinese light soy sauce
2 Tbsp	25 mL	rice vinegar
2 tsp	10 mL	sesame oil
2 Tbsp	25 mL	diced green onion
1		egg white, beaten
2 Tbsp	25 mL	cornstarch
		freshly ground black pepper to taste
30		dumpling wrappers*
		water (as needed)
		fish roe (for garnish)*

*Dumpling wrappers and fish roe are now available at most supermarkets. You'll find a small jar of fish roe in the canned tuna section of the supermarket. Both items are also available at Asian supermarkets.

To make the dipping sauce, combine the ingredients in a large bowl and mix them together. Cover and refrigerate it until it's needed.

To make the dumplings, dice the shrimp. Combine the shrimp, pork, soy sauce, vinegar, sesame oil, green onion, egg white and cornstarch in a large bowl and mix well. Season the mixture with pepper.

Place 1 Tbsp (15 mL) of the filling in the center of each dumpling wrapper. Gather up all the edges of the wrapper around the filling, so the wrapper is like a cup holding the mixture. Press the bottom of the cup on a flat surface to flatten each wrapper. Using a little water, smooth the surface. Coat a large plate with a little oil. Place the dumplings on the plate. Cover them and refrigerate them until they're needed, but no longer than 2 hours.

continued on next page

Spray the bamboo steamer with nonstick cooking spray. Place the steamer over a skillet filled with 2 inches (5 cm) of water. Place the dumplings in the steamer. Bring the water to a boil over high heat. Place the bamboo steamer over the skillet of boiling water. Cover and steam the dumplings for 15 minutes.

Remove them from the heat and place a dollop of fish roe in the center of each dumpling. Place the dumplings on a serving platter and serve them warm, with the dipping sauce.

building blocks
The predominant building block is the heat and spice in the dipping sauce. Choose a sparkling wine with sweetness to offset them.

flavors
Choose a sparkling wine with lemon-lime flavors to work with the lime flavor of the dipping sauce.

zhen zhu wan zi with lime dipping sauce

Zhen Zhu Wan Zi refers to Chinese pearl meatballs, also called porcupine or rice-studded meatballs. No matter what you choose to call them, they're interesting to look at, easy to make and delicious.

Serves 4–6 (makes 24 meatballs)

Lime dipping sauce:

2 Tbsp	25 mL	freshly squeezed lime juice
¼ cup	50 mL	Chinese light soy sauce
½ tsp	2 mL	chili paste with fried garlic*

Meatballs:

1 cup	250 mL	jasmine rice
2–4		outer bok choy leaves, plus extra for serving
4		scallions
1		egg
½ cup	125 mL	diced canned water chestnuts
1 Tbsp	15 mL	each cornstarch, rice vinegar and sesame oil
1 tsp	5 mL	sugar
½ tsp	2 mL	chili paste
1 lb	500 g	ground pork
		sea salt to taste
		freshly ground black pepper to taste
		water (as needed)
		toothpicks

*Chili paste with fried garlic is available at Asian supermarkets.

Combine the dipping sauce ingredients in a small bowl. Cover the sauce with plastic wrap and chill it until it's needed. Place the rice in a bowl. Cover it with hot water and soak it until it's needed. Set a skillet filled with cold water on the stove and place a bamboo or metal steamer in the skillet. Line the steamer with the bok choy leaves.

To make the meatballs, combine the scallions, egg, water chestnuts, cornstarch, rice vinegar, sesame oil, sugar and chili paste in a food processor or blender. Purée and transfer it to a bowl. Add the ground pork and season the meatball mixture with salt and pepper. Mix it well, then roll it into balls. Drain the rice and transfer it to a shallow dish. Coat the meatballs with the damp rice.

Bring the water in the skillet to a boil. Place batches of the meatballs in the bamboo steamer and steam them until the pork is cooked through, about 25 minutes. Insert a toothpick in each of the meatballs and place them on a platter lined with more bok choy leaves. Serve them with the dipping sauce.

building blocks
The predominant building blocks are sourness and saltiness from the lime juice and fish sauce in the dipping sauce. A brut sparkling wine has enough sourness to match and offsets the saltiness.

flavors
Choose a brut sparkling wine with citrus tones to match the flavor of the lime.

orgasmic
appetizers
to pair
with crisp,
dry whites

Crisp, dry whites

PREDOMINANT BUILDING BLOCKS:

Sourness and fruitiness.

FLAVORS:

Lemon, lime, gooseberry, grapefruit, green apple, pineapple.

Other flavors include floral, grassy and mineral-like.

WINES PRODUCED IN THE CRISP, DRY WHITE STYLE

- Wines produced in this style tend to have a natural backbone of crisp acidity with light to medium body.

- They're considered good food wines as this acidity cleans the palate between bites.

- This is a popular wine style at the moment, its most famous wine being Sauvignon Blanc, which is produced in both warm and cool climates.

- Crisp, dry whites can be inexpensive and are ideal as picnic and barbecue wines, or sophisticated companions to gourmet fare like caviar or oysters on the half shell.

- Their best food matches highlight summer vegetables, such as fresh tomatoes, spinach, mixed greens, artichokes and asparagus. They also work with sour ingredients like goat cheese, feta and yogurt.

The regions at right are stylistically noted for producing crisp, dry white wines.

REGIONS

sauvignon blanc
Canada (British Columbia, Ontario)
Chile (Casablanca Valley)
France (Bordeaux, Languedoc, Loire)
Italy (Friuli)
New Zealand
South Africa
Spain (Penedés, Rueda)
United States (California)

dry riesling
Canada (British Columbia, Ontario)
France (Alsace)
Germany
United States (Oregon, Washington State)

others
Aligoté — Canada (Ontario)
Chenin Blanc —South Africa, United States (California)
Cortese di Gavi — Italy (Piedmont)
DOC Frascati — Italy (Latium/Lazio)
DOC Vernaccia di San Gimignano — Italy (Florence)
Grüner Veltliner — Austria
Muscadet — France (Loire)
Orvieto — Italy (Umbria)
Verdicchio dei Castelli di Jesi — Italy (The Marches)
Vinho Verde — Portugal (Vinho Verde)
Viognier — France (Côtes du Rhône)
Viura — Spain (Rioja)

tuna, green olive & caper spread on toasts

I served this appetizer at an afternoon barbecue by the lake. My super-tasting friends prefer a subtle anchovy flavor (one to two anchovies), while my nontasting pals like a prominent anchovy flavor (four to six). You'll have to decide on the amount of salty umami (anchovies) you prefer.

Serves 4–6 (makes 24 toasts)

Toasts:

1		baked baguette, frozen
		corn oil (for frying)
		sea salt to taste

Spread:

1		6 oz (170 g) can of tuna
4		anchovies, minced
3		cloves garlic, minced
½ cup	125 mL	pitted and sliced green olives
2 Tbsp	25 mL	capers, finely chopped
2 Tbsp	25 mL	freshly squeezed lemon juice
4 oz	125 g	cream cheese
		sea salt to taste
		freshly ground black pepper to taste
		capers (for garnish)
		finely chopped fresh Italian parsley (for garnish)

Using a serrated knife, slice the frozen baguette into 24 thin slices. Heat the oil in a large skillet until hot but not smoking. Fry the baguette slices until they're golden, about 15 seconds per side. Drain them on paper towel. Season them with salt.

To make the spread, combine the tuna, anchovies, garlic, olives, capers and lemon juice in a food processor or blender. While pulsating the blade, slowly add the cream cheese, turning the mixture into a smooth paste. Transfer it to a bowl. Season it with salt and pepper.

Spread the paste onto the toasts. Sprinkle the toasts with fresh parsley and capers and place them on a serving platter. Serve them at room temperature.

building blocks
The predominant building block is saltiness from the anchovies and capers. A crisp, dry white wine has enough sourness to offset the saltiness.

flavors
Choose a crisp, dry white with citrus notes to complement the tuna, anchovies and capers.

capers & wine

Capers are the flower buds that grow on a bush on plantations in countries such as Turkey, Spain, France and Italy. French capers are petite and tend to have a delicate texture and possess high acidity. They're considered to be of exceptional quality. They must be hand-harvested, due to their tiny size, which is why they're so expensive.

Italian capers are larger, and in Spain they're larger still—the size of olives. The closed buds are harvested, withered and pickled in salt water or vinegar. This gives them a sharp, sour and bitingly salty flavor. Due to their saltiness, Spanish capers should be rinsed before using. They add flavor to vegetables, fish, seafood, meats and sauces. Their bright green color gives a dish visual variety.

Cold pasta with fresh tomatoes, olives and capers drizzled with a white balsamic vinaigrette is delicious. Capers also harmonize with smoked salmon (salty) drizzled with lemon juice. These tiny buds also complement some meats, such as veal. How about veal scallops with capers, dill and vermouth?

The sour and salty flavor of capers is scrumptious in Sauce Ravigote. This classic French white sauce combines white wine, cream, white wine vinegar, butter, shallots, chervil, tarragon, chives and capers. The sour and salty flavor of the capers contrasts nicely with the rich elements of the butter and cream.

Crisp, dry white wines and brut sparkling wines are capers' best match. Recipes using capers tend to clash with red wine. Ideal wines for dishes with capers are Sauvignon Blanc, dry Riesling, Vinho Verde and Orvieto.

Capers are sometimes added to dishes to offset the sweetness of fruits such as raisins. Their sour and salty taste offsets the fruits' intense sweetness. Pair these dishes with wines offering sweetness, such as a sparkling wine that isn't too dry, or an off-dry white wine.

Hot and spicy dishes can benefit from capers, as well—imagine crab cakes with a dollop of wasabi and caper mayonnaise. Pair hot and spicy dishes to wines offering sweetness.

scampi stuffed with goat cheese & wrapped in prosciutto

I cannot count how many times I've relied upon this recipe to please guests and make a good impression. It serves as a great starter whether you're hosting a private party, a fundraising event or a wedding.

Serves 4–6 (makes 18 scampi)

8 oz	250 g	goat cheese, at room temperature
2 tsp	10 mL	finely chopped fresh chives
		sea salt to taste
		freshly ground black pepper to taste
18		large shrimp, peeled and butterflied with their tails on
12		shaved slices of prosciutto strips (¼ inch/5 mm)
		olive oil (as needed)

Blend the cheese and the chives in a medium bowl. Season the mixture to taste with salt and pepper.

Season the shrimp with salt and pepper. Press 1 tsp (5 mL) of the cheese mixture in the cavity of each shrimp. Wrap a piece of prosciutto tightly around each shrimp.

Heat the oil in a skillet. When the oil is hot, add the stuffed shrimp and sear them for 2 to 3 minutes on each side, or until the shrimp turn pink, their tails curl toward their bodies and the prosciutto is crisp. Remove the shrimp from the pan and place them on a large plate. Serve them hot.

building blocks
The predominant building blocks of this appetizer are sourness from the goat cheese and saltiness from the prosciutto. A crisp, dry white with sourness harmonizes with the goat cheese and offsets the saltiness.

flavors
Choose a crisp, dry white with herbal tones to bring out the subtle flavor of the chives.

mini treasures

Caviar is said to increase blood flow and is therefore believed to be an aphrodisiac. But you certainly don't want to eat too much of it as it's high in cholesterol and salt. This appetizer calls for just a smidgen to add a little saltiness to balance the tangy flavor of the cream cheese. A piping bag will make the cream cheese topping look elegant.

Serves 4–6 (makes 16 mini potato skins)

Mini potato skins:

4		mini white potatoes
4		mini red potatoes
		corn oil (for deep-frying)

Filling:

8 oz	250 g	cream cheese, at room temperature
2 tsp	10 mL	finely chopped fresh mint
		sea salt to taste
		freshly ground black pepper to taste
16		small, fresh basil leaves
¼ cup	50 mL	caviar of choice

Wash the potatoes. Cut a thin slice off the top and bottom of each potato to make a flat surface for it to sit on. Cut the potatoes in half, parallel to the previous 2 cuts. Using a melon baller, scoop out the insides of the potatoes, leaving about ¼ inch (5 mm) of flesh with the skin. Fill a large pot with boiling, salted water. Add the potatoes. Cook the potatoes for 15 minutes or until they're *al dente*. Fill a large bowl with cold water. Remove the potatoes with a slotted spoon and transfer them to the cold water "bath" to stop them from cooking further.

Heat the oil to 375°F (190°C) in a deep-fryer or a large, deep pot. Deep-fry the potato skins for 2 to 3 minutes, or until they're golden brown. Remove the skins from the oil using a slotted spoon. Drain them on paper towel. Let them cool.

Combine the cream cheese, mint, salt and pepper in a small bowl. Transfer this mixture to a piping bag. Set a basil leaf to one side inside each potato skin. (When the cream cheese is piped into the potato skins, you want to see the green leaf.) Pipe about 1 tsp (5 mL) of the cream cheese topping into each potato skin. Add ¼ tsp (1 mL) of caviar. Serve the potato skins at room temperature or chilled.

building blocks
The predominant building block is saltiness from the caviar. A crisp, dry white has enough sourness to offset the saltiness.

flavors
Choose a crisp, dry white with citrus notes to complement the flavor of the caviar.

sassy mexicali salsa

This salsa is at its best when it's prepared just before serving. Even with the lime juice, the avocados begin to brown after a few hours, making it less attractive. If you must make this in advance, mix together the tomatoes, onion and garlic. Prepare the dressing in advance. Then, at the last minute, cut the avocados and add them to the salsa. Add the dressing last.

Serves 4–6

2		ripe avocados, peeled, pitted and diced
3		medium yellow tomatoes, diced
1		small red onion, finely chopped
2		cloves garlic, minced
¼ cup	50 mL	freshly squeezed lime juice
¼ cup	50 mL	olive oil
¼ cup	50 mL	finely chopped fresh cilantro
½ tsp	2 mL	ground cumin
		sea salt to taste
		freshly ground black pepper to taste
		tortilla chips

Combine the avocados, tomatoes, red onion and garlic in a medium bowl and toss them together. Combine the lime juice and olive oil in another small bowl. Whisk them together. Fold in the cilantro.

Place the cumin in a dry skillet over low heat. Heat it until the spice is aromatic, then scrape it into the lime juice dressing. Whisk the dressing. Season the salsa with salt and pepper. Add the dressing to the salsa ingredients but do not overmix. Pour the salsa into a bowl and serve it immediately with tortilla chips.

building blocks
The predominant building block in this recipe is sourness, due to the yellow tomatoes and lime juice. A crisp, dry white has enough sourness to match.

flavors
Choose a crisp, dry white with citrus notes to complement the lime flavor.

the good, the bad & the ugly

One of the many joys of drinking wine is being able to articulate what you detect in its bouquet. Fruit wines are supposed to smell like the fruit from which they're made, but wine made from grapes is not supposed to smell like grapes. A grape-y scent is undesirable. Wines are supposed to develop a wide array of aromas that range from fruits and flowers to earth and spice.

Cat pee is an aroma that's certainly one of the most confusing terms the experts use to describe wine. The fragrance of cat pee in a crisp, dry white like Sauvignon Blanc grown in the Marlborough region of New Zealand is a good thing. If it smells like cat pee and gooseberries, you're no doubt sipping a wine that exemplifies the true character of its varietal when it's grown in this beautiful country. In fact, so desirable are cat pee and gooseberry as aromas in Sauvignon Blanc that New Zealand's Cooper's Creek winery makes a quaffer called "Cat's Pee on a Gooseberry Bush."

Where does the aroma of cat pee come from? Pyrazines are the cat pee culprit. Pyrazines are compounds found in many fruits and vegetables. They're found in ripened Sauvignon Blanc grapes grown in Marlborough. The aroma of pyrazine in a New Zealand Sauvignon Blanc is wonderful, while the identical smell in an Ontario version is horrible. In Ontario wines, this smell is caused by a ladybug infestation in the vineyard—a very bad thing. California Sauvignon Blanc has low pyrazine levels. In Bordeaux, Sauvignon Blanc is often blended with the grapes of Semillon and Muscadelle to eliminate the pyrazine smell altogether. So if you find the cat pee nose offensive, drink California Sauvignon Blanc. If you enjoy Marlborough Sauvignon Blanc, but dislike the term, then simply describe the wine in another way. If you say the wine's aroma smells of

pyrazine, your guests will no doubt roll their eyes and think you snobby. You could say that the Sauvignon Blanc has an aroma reminiscent of the southern end of a northbound cat. Another "delightful" wine aroma is that of gasoline. The great Rieslings of Germany have a nose swirling with gasoline or diesel. Other yummy terms are manure, mineral-like, barnyard, tobacco, cigar, cedar, bacon, mushroom and sweat. Yes, sweat! Our lovely Sauvignon Blanc can possess the aroma of armpits, but when it translates into flavor, that's a good thing.

While many wine lovers experience the aromas of cat pee and sweat as positive, the description "wet dog" is meant to be negative. Canada originally earned its unworthy reputation for producing inferior wine from its indigenous Vitis labrusca grapes. The Concord grape variety is one of them. The Concord grape makes for delicious juice and jelly, but gives wine the smell of a wet dog. Wet dog is a bad thing. Thank goodness Canadian winemakers are now producing world-class wines from Vitis vinifera grapes, such as Chardonnay, Riesling and Pinot Noir.

Bad aromas are almost tolerable when compared to wine "faults." Some nasty aromas are a result not of the varietal and terroir, but of poor wine-making practices. If a winemaker uses an excessive amount of sulfur dioxide, the resulting wine can have aromas of mothballs and burnt rubber. If a wine possesses too much ethyl acetate, it will smell like nail polish remover. Vinegar can be a lovely smell in food, but not in wine. The aroma of vinegar in wine means it's turned to acetic acid and is therefore over the hill. That's a truly unfortunate thing.

Maybe New Zealand Sauvignon Blanc is for cat lovers only.

salt lover's canapés

My good friends Garry and Eleanor Humphries made these fabulous toasts for my husband and me one sunny summer afternoon. We all found them highly addictive, no doubt due to the umami-rich, salty ingredient, anchovies.

Serves 4–6 (makes 24 canapés)

building blocks
The predominant building block is saltiness from the anchovies. The sourness of a crisp, dry white offsets the saltiness.

flavors
Choose a crisp, dry white with citrus flavors to harmonize with the licorice-like taste of sweet fennel.

2		small red peppers
1		small yellow pepper
		vegetable oil (as needed)

Anchovy butter:

1 Tbsp	15 mL	sweet fennel seeds
½ cup	125 mL	unsalted butter, softened
6–9		flat anchovy fillets, patted dry and minced
1 tsp	5 mL	freshly squeezed lemon juice
		freshly ground black pepper to taste
24		diagonal slices or rounds of whole wheat baguette, ¼ inch (5 mm) thick

Preheat the oven to 450°F (230°C). Cut the peppers in half and place them on a well-oiled baking sheet. Coat the peppers with oil. Roast them for 25 to 30 minutes or until the peppers are blackened. Remove them from the oven. Place the peppers in a paper bag and let them stand for 20 minutes. Peel and seed the peppers. Cut the roasted peppers lengthwise into ⅛-inch-wide (3 mm) strips. Set them aside.

To make the anchovy butter, toast the fennel seeds in a dry skillet over medium heat, shaking the skillet frequently, until the fennel is golden, 3 to 4 minutes. Transfer the fennel to a bowl and let it cool.

Using a coffee grinder or a mortar and pestle, grind the fennel seeds. Place the butter in a bowl with the ground fennel. Add the anchovies, lemon juice and pepper. Combine the mixture well.

Preheat the broiler. Broil the baguette slices until golden, about 1 to 2 minutes, on a rimmed baking sheet sprayed with nonstick cooking spray. Turn the slices over and spread them generously with the anchovy butter. Broil the toasts until the butter is golden and bubbling, about 1 minute. Transfer the toasts to a serving platter. Top each toast with a strip each of the yellow and red peppers. Serve them warm or at room temperature.

geisha carrot dip with crisp vegetables

I obtained this recipe from famous chef Ritchie Kukle—he was the private chef to Melanie Griffith and Don Johnson for five years. Chef Ritchie also cooked for their famous guests, including Sylvester Stallone, Robert Wagner and Goldie Hawn. Ronald Perelman (the American corporate "turnaround" specialist) was another of Ritchie's private clients—Perelman's guests included Martha Stewart, Billy Joel, Shirley MacLaine and Antonio Banderas. This dip is brilliantly simple and brilliantly orgasmic!

Serves 4–6

1¼ cups	300 mL	peeled and cooked carrots
¼ cup	50 mL	finely chopped Spanish onion
1 inch	2.5 cm	piece fresh ginger, grated
½ cup	125 mL	Japanese light soy sauce
½ cup	125 mL	rice vinegar
½ cup	125 mL	vegetable oil

Place all the ingredients in a blender and purée them until the mixture is smooth. Adjust the amount of ginger, soy sauce and vinegar to taste. Cover and chill the dip until it's needed, up to 24 hours. Serve it with cherry tomatoes, sliced cucumber and celery.

building blocks
The predominant building block is saltiness from the soy sauce. The sourness of a crisp, dry white nicely offsets the saltiness.

flavors
Choose a crisp, dry white with herbal notes to complement the flavors in the fresh vegetables.

roasted red pepper dip

The Shish-Kabob Hut in Peterborough is renowned for its authentic Greek cuisine, which includes its famous Hot Pepper and Feta Dip. Unfortunately, friend and owner Don Vassiliadis couldn't give me his family recipe for this book as it's one of the restaurant's top-selling dishes, a recipe that has been in the family for generations. But Don gave me some great suggestions so that I could develop my own version, inspired by the original. The key to this dip is to use quality Greek feta.

Serves 4–6

6		whole wheat pitas
Dip:		
4		red bell peppers
		olive oil (as needed)
2		garlic cloves, peeled
1 lb	500 g	Greek feta
8 oz	250 g	cream cheese
		sea salt to taste
		freshly ground black pepper to taste

Preheat the oven to 375°F (190°C). Separate the layers of each pita with a serrated knife. Stack 2 or 3 layers together and cut the pita into quarters, or eighths if you prefer. Spread the wedges out on 2 large rimmed baking sheets sprayed with nonstick cooking spray. Bake them for about 20 minutes or until the pieces are golden. Cool them completely.

To make the dip, preheat the oven to broil. Place the peppers on a rimmed baking sheet sprayed with nonstick cooking spray. Coat the peppers with oil. Broil them for about 15 minutes. Put the peppers in a paper bag for 20 minutes. Let them cool. Peel, seed and quarter the peppers.

Put the peppers in a food processor or blender with the garlic, feta and cream cheese. Slowly add the oil, with the motor running, until the mixture has a creamy consistency. Transfer it to a serving bowl. Season it with salt and pepper. Cover and refrigerate it for 3 hours, or, for best results, chill it overnight. Pour the dip into a bowl and serve it with the toasted pita wedges.

building blocks
The predominant building block in this dip is saltiness. A crisp, dry white has enough sourness to nicely offset the saltiness.

flavors
Choose a crisp, dry white with citrus tones to draw out the subtle, fruity flavor of the roasted red peppers.

orgasmic appetizers to pair with well-balanced, medium-bodied, smooth whites

Well-balanced, medium-bodied, smooth whites

PREDOMINANT BUILDING BLOCKS:

Balance of sourness and fruitiness with some fattiness.

FLAVORS:

Light and peachy to lush and tropical.

Other flavors include nutty, mineral-like and floral.

WINES PRODUCED IN THE WELL-BALANCED, MEDIUM-BODIED STYLE

- Cooler regions that produce quality wines in this style are Canada, Oregon, Long Island, Burgundy and Northern Italy, to name a few.

- Warmer regions such as Chile can also produce wines in this style. Super-tasters often enjoy these wines because there are no in-your-face building blocks that stand out on the palate.

- Wines in this style have generally been fermented in stainless steel tanks and may go through a secondary fermentation called malolactic fermentation. This converts some of the harsh malic acid to creamy lactic acid, softening the wine.

- These wines may spend a short time aging in oak barrels.

- Their best food matches are spring and fall vegetables such as carrots, parsnips, cabbage and onions.

- Cheeses with soft character work best here, including havarti, young to medium-aged cheddar, young brie and young Camembert.

The regions at right are stylistically noted for producing well-balanced, medium-bodied smooth whites.

REGIONS

chardonnay
Argentina
Canada (British Columbia, Ontario)
Chile
France (Burgundy)
Italy (Northern)
South Africa
United States (Northern California, Oregon, Washington State)

chenin blanc
Canada (British Columbia, Ontario)
Chile
France (Loire)
South Africa
United States (California)

pinot blanc
Austria
Canada (British Columbia, Ontario)
France (Alsace)
Italy

pinot grigio
Canada (Ontario)
Italy (Northern, Central)

pinot gris
Canada (British Columbia, Ontario)
Switzerland

sémillon
Australia
France (Bordeaux)

sémillon/chardonnay
Australia

others
Dry Gewürztraminer — France (Alsace)
Dry Vouvray — France (Loire)
Sancerre — France (Loire)
Soave Classico — Italy (Veneto)

crab & shrimp cakes

When I'm hosting a dinner party, I like to include in the appetizer menu interesting new flavors and also an ol' reliable or two like a crab cake featuring delicate and familiar flavors. This is to make sure my super-tasting friends will also enjoy themselves.

Serves 4–6
(makes 6 crab cakes)

½ lb	250 g	freshly shelled crabmeat*
½ lb	250 g	shrimp, peeled and deveined, finely chopped
½ bunch		fresh cilantro with stems removed, chopped
3		green onions, finely chopped
¼ cup	50 mL	mayonnaise
1 cup	250 mL	dried breadcrumbs
		sea salt to taste
		freshly ground black pepper to taste
		sour cream (for garnish)
		cilantro sprigs (for garnish)

*If fresh crabmeat is unavailable, use a canned version.

Preheat the oven to 350°F (180°C). Drain the crabmeat thoroughly. Mix the crab with the shrimp, cilantro, green onions, mayonnaise and breadcrumbs in a large bowl. Season the mixture with salt and pepper. Divide the crabmeat into 6 balls and press them into patties about 2 inches (5 cm) in diameter and ½ inch (1 cm) thick. Place the patties on a plate. Cover and refrigerate them until they're needed.

Brown the patties on both sides in a dry skillet over medium heat. Transfer the patties to a rimmed baking sheet sprayed with nonstick cooking spray. Bake them for 5 to 7 minutes, or until they're cooked through. Top them with a dollop of sour cream and sprigs of fresh cilantro and serve them immediately.

building blocks
The predominant building block is medium fattiness due to the richness of the seafood and the mayonnaise. A well-balanced, medium-bodied white has enough weight to match.

flavors
Choose a well-balanced, medium-bodied white with citrus notes to harmonize with the flavors of the crab and shrimp.

chicken & goat cheese pound cake

The texture of this appetizer is much like that of a pound cake. It's technically considered a pâté en croûte. *Don't let the texture fool you. It's tasty.*

Serves 4–6

2 lb	1 kg	boneless, skinless chicken breasts, cubed
2		eggs
¼ cup	50 mL	chopped fresh dill
½ cup	125 mL	chopped fresh tarragon
2 tsp	10 mL	sea salt
½ tsp	2 mL	nutmeg
¼ tsp	1 mL	cayenne pepper
3 cups	750 mL	heavy cream
8 oz	250 g	crumbled goat cheese
½ cup	125 mL	finely chopped and re-hydrated sun-dried tomatoes
		toasted baguette slices

Preheat the oven to 350°F (180°C). Place the chicken cubes, eggs, dill, tarragon, salt, nutmeg and cayenne in a food processor or a blender. While the machine pulsates, add the cream and purée the mixture until it's smooth.

Pour half the mixture into a nonstick loaf pan. Top it with half the crumbled goat cheese. Sprinkle that with half the sun-dried tomato pieces. Pour another layer of the chicken mixture into the pan, about a quarter of the remaining mixture. Add the remaining goat cheese and sun-dried tomatoes. Top with the remainder of the mixture. Set the loaf pan in a larger pan on the middle rack of the oven. Pour enough boiling water into the larger pan to come about halfway up the sides of the loaf pan. Bake the pâté for 1 hour or until a knife inserted into the middle of the pâté comes out clean. Remove it from the oven. Let it stand until it's cool. Cover the pâté and refrigerate it for about 2 hours. Serve the pâté on a plate surrounded by slices of toast, or spread it on toasts in advance.

building blocks
The predominant building block is sourness and fattiness, due to the goat cheese and cream. A well-balanced, medium-bodied white has enough sourness and weight to match.

flavors
Choose a well-balanced, medium-bodied white with mineral tones to highlight the subtle flavors of the dill and tarragon.

smoked salmon pancakes with chive cream

The participants in my wine class at Fleming College gave the thumbs-up to this recipe. Its flavors are simple and delicate, pleasing the non-tasters, medium-tasters and super-tasters.

Serves 4–6 (makes 12 pancakes)

½ cup	125 mL	all-purpose flour
1½ tsp	7 mL	baking powder
1		egg, beaten
2 Tbsp	25 mL	milk (more if needed)
1 tsp	5 mL	sour cream
		corn oil (for frying)

Herbed cream:

½ cup	125 mL	sour cream
2 Tbsp	25 mL	mayonnaise
1 Tbsp	15 mL	freshly squeezed lemon juice
1 Tbsp	15 mL	finely chopped fresh chives
1 Tbsp	15 mL	finely chopped fresh mint
¼ lb	125 g	smoked salmon, sliced
12		strips of lemon peel

Combine the flour and baking powder in a medium bowl and mix them together well. Make a well in the mixture. Add the egg, milk and sour cream, then mix until the batter is smooth and free of lumps. Set it aside.

Heat the oil in a large skillet over medium heat. Using a spoon, pour 1 tsp (5 mL) of the batter into the skillet. Make 12 pancakes, 2 inches (5 cm) in diameter and not too thick. When the tops of the pancakes begin to bubble, which may take about 30 seconds, flip the pancakes and cook the other side, about 30 seconds.

To make the herbed cream, combine the sour cream, mayonnaise, lemon juice, chives and mint in a medium bowl, mixing well. Place 1 tsp (5 mL) of herbed cream on each pancake. Roll up or simply place a slice of smoked salmon on the cream. Garnish the pancakes with the lemon peel. Serve the pancakes chilled.

building blocks

The predominant building blocks are sourness from the lemon and sour cream and saltiness from the smoked salmon. A well-balanced, medium-bodied white has enough sourness to work with the lemon and sour cream, but enough body to stand up to the pancake and smoked salmon.

flavors

Choose a well-balanced, medium-bodied white with citrus flavor to match the flavor of the lemon and mayonnaise.

artichoke & parmigiano-reggiano dip

The simplest recipes can offer great taste. This is an example of a dip that can be made in a few minutes and yet will have your guests moaning in delight. Parmigiano-Reggiano represents both basic and synergistic umami.

Serves 4–6

2 cups	500 mL	artichoke hearts, chopped
1 cup	250 mL	freshly grated Parmigiano-Reggiano
1 cup	250 mL	mayonnaise
3		cloves garlic, minced
½ tsp	2 mL	freshly squeezed lemon juice
		sea salt to taste
		freshly ground black pepper to taste
		flatbread

Preheat the oven to 350°F (180°C). Combine all the ingredients in a large bowl and mix them together well. Transfer the mixture to a heatproof casserole dish. Bake it for 20 minutes or until the dip is hot. Serve it with pieces of flatbread.

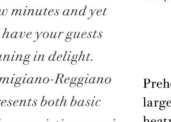

building blocks
The predominant building block is saltiness from the Parmigiano and creaminess from the mayonnaise. A well-balanced, medium-bodied white has enough sourness to offset the cheese and enough body to match the weight of the mayonnaise.

flavors
Choose a well-balanced, medium-bodied white with herbal notes to complement the flavor of the artichokes.

spinach-artichoke wonton cups

I love working with wonton wrappers. They're easy to use and, when baked or fried, offer a crunchy texture that complements many flavors.

Serves 4–6 (makes 36 cups)

36		wonton wrappers
¼ cup	50 mL	butter, melted
1		can artichoke hearts (about 8 oz/250 g), drained and chopped
1 cup	250 mL	steamed fresh spinach
1 cup	250 mL	freshly grated medium cheddar cheese
½ cup	125 mL	freshly grated Parmigiano-Reggiano
8 oz	250 g	cream cheese
2		cloves garlic, minced

Preheat the oven to 350°F (180°C). Spray a 24-cup mini muffin pan with nonstick cooking spray. Press a wonton wrapper into each cup, making a shell. Brush the inside of the cups with melted butter. Bake them for 5 to 7 minutes, or until the shells are golden. Remove them from the heat, then remove the shells from the pan. Place them on a wire rack to cool. Repeat with the remaining wrappers, making 36 cups in total.

Meanwhile, combine the artichoke hearts, spinach, cheddar cheese, Parmigiano, cream cheese and garlic in a medium bowl and mix them together well. Fill the wonton cups with about 1 tsp (5 mL) of the mixture. Place the filled cups on a rimmed baking sheet sprayed with nonstick cooking spray and bake them for another 5 minutes, or until heated through. Serve them immediately. Use any remaining filling on toasts or make more wonton cups.

building blocks
The predominant building block is moderate fattiness from the cheeses. A well-balanced, medium-bodied white has enough weight to match.

flavors
Choose a well-balanced medium-bodied white with apple and pear character to harmonize with the flavor of the cheddar cheese.

stuffed baguette with spicy ham spread

Sharon Aubie, one of the participants in my wine course at Fleming College, brought this spread to our class to sample. It's a family favorite, handed down through generations. At first I was apprehensive about trying a recipe that uses canned ham, because I prefer fresh ingredients. But when the class and I tried this spread, we were all pleasantly surprised by the recipe's simplicity and wonderful flavors. We all agreed this traditional Aubie spread deserved to be celebrated in this cookbook. I've added the baguette presentation for a new twist.

*Serves 4–6
(makes 12 rounds)*

24 oz	750 g	cream cheese, at room temperature (three 8 oz/250 g packages)
3		5.5 oz (156 g) tins flaked ham
¼ cup	50 mL	sour cream
1 Tbsp	15 mL	Worcestershire sauce
1 Tbsp	15 mL	freshly squeezed lemon juice
1 tsp	5 mL	cayenne
		freshly ground black pepper to taste
1		medium onion, finely chopped
1		baguette
		pimento-stuffed olives (for garnish)

Put the cream cheese in a medium bowl. Open and drain the ham, fork the flakes of ham into small pieces and add them to the cream cheese. Add the sour cream, Worcestershire, lemon juice and cayenne and mix the ingredients together well. Season with pepper. Fold in the onion. Cover and refrigerate for several hours or overnight.

Slice off the ends of the baguette. Cut the baguette in thirds so you have 3 loaves, each about 6 inches (15 cm) long. Use a long, serrated knife to hollow out the inside of the loaf, leaving a thin-crust casing. Stand 1 end of the hollow loaf on a flat work surface. Tightly pack the empty loaf with ham spread, using a spoon. Repeat with the other 2 sections of the loaf. Wrap the stuffed loaves in foil and refrigerate them for several hours to set.

Before serving, slice the bread into ½-inch (1 cm) rounds. Use a serrated knife for clean, straight edges. Quarter the olives. Place a quarter-olive in the center of each baguette round. Arrange the rounds on a platter. Cover and refrigerate them until they're needed.

building blocks
The predominant building blocks are some fattiness due to the cream cheese and a hint of saltiness from the ham. A well-balanced, medium-bodied white has enough weight to stand up to the fattiness in the cream cheese. The wine's sourness nicely offsets the saltiness of the ham.

flavors
Choose a well-balanced, medium-bodied white with some tropical flavor to harmonize with the flavor of the ham.

wild mushroom wellington

Stargazers on the Thames is a delightful restaurant in Pain Court, Ontario. Wild Mushroom Wellington has already established itself as a favorite among the restaurant's valued clientele. Wine Spectator *magazine has recognized Stargazers for its excellent wine list, as well.*

Serves 4–6
(makes 8 Wellingtons)

¼ cup	50 mL	extra virgin olive oil
1 Tbsp	15 mL	minced garlic
2 tsp	10 mL	pesto
4		medium Portobello mushrooms, stems removed, cut in half
½		large eggplant, peeled and sliced
1		red bell pepper, julienned
1		zucchini, sliced
1		medium Vidalia onion, sliced
2 Tbsp	25 mL	balsamic vinegar
2		sheets frozen puff pastry, thawed
		sea salt to taste
		freshly ground black pepper to taste
1 cup	250 mL	crumbled goat cheese, at room temperature
¼ cup	50 mL	melted butter

Preheat the oven to 375°F (190°C). Combine the olive oil, garlic, pesto and mushrooms in a mixing bowl, then remove the mushrooms from the marinade, reserving the marinade. Set the mushrooms on a rimmed baking sheet sprayed with nonstick cooking spray. Bake them for 18 to 20 minutes, or until they're tender. Cool the mushrooms completely.

Start the barbecue. Grill the eggplant, pepper, zucchini and onion over low heat until they're cooked through. Then dice the hot, grilled vegetables and toss them in the reserved marinade, along with the balsamic vinegar. Drain off the excess marinade and cool the vegetables completely.

Cut the puff pastry sheets into 8 pieces each, making 16 squares in total. Place 1 Portobello mushroom half (gill side facing upward) on each square of puff pastry. Top the mushrooms with 2 Tbsp (25 mL) of the diced vegetables and season them lightly with salt and pepper. Top the vegetables with about 2 Tbsp (25 mL) of goat cheese. Place another pastry square on top. Seal the bottom and top squares of the pastry, crimping the edges with a fork. Repeat until you've made 8 mushroom Wellingtons. Brush the top of the pastry with melted butter. Put the Wellingtons on a rimmed baking sheet sprayed with nonstick cooking spray. Bake them for 3 to 5 minutes, watching closely, until the pastry is hot and golden brown.

building blocks
The predominant building block is sourness, due to the goat cheese and balsamic vinegar and the fattiness of the puff pastry. A well-balanced, medium-bodied white wine offers the harmony of fruitiness and sourness to match.

flavors
Choose a well-balanced, medium-bodied white with herbal tones to complement the flavor of the vegetables.

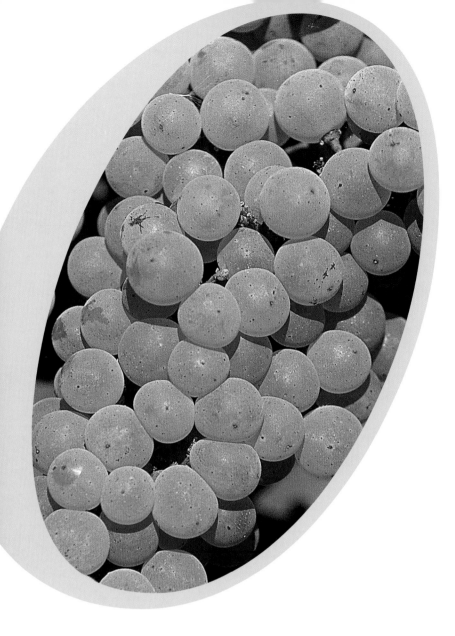

*orgasmic
appetizers
to pair
with big,
fat whites*

*b*ig, *fat whites*

PREDOMINANT BUILDING BLOCKS:
Fattiness with some sourness and fruitiness.

FLAVORS:
Buttery, creamy, oily, nutty, toasty, oaky and spicy; subtle fruity and floral flavors.

WINES PRODUCED IN THE BIG, FAT WHITE STYLE

- Wines in this style are often fermented and aged in oak barrels and undergo a secondary, malolactic fermentation that converts some of the apple-like acid to a softer lactic acid. These processes give wines in this style their identifiable complexity, with rich, creamy texture and buttery aromas and flavors.

- Big, fat whites are always full-bodied, usually with high alcohol.

- Medium-tasters and nontasters, who love bold, unique flavors like vanilla, oak and woody-ness, generally love this wine style.

- Big, fat whites are considered to be "out of style" at the moment. However, they have an important place in the realm of food pairing, as many fatty dishes require a white wine with this weight, complexity and creamy nature.

- Best food matches for wines in this style are high-fat and deep-fried foods, fatty cheeses and heavy vegetables such as shrimp tempura, double- and triple-cream brie and potatoes. You can also pair big, fat whites with Alfredo-, butter-, pesto- and olive oil-based sauces.

The regions at right are stylistically noted for producing big, fat whites.

REGIONS

oaked chardonnay
Australia
Canada (British Columbia, Ontario)
Chile
New Zealand
South Africa
United States (California — Napa, Russian River, Sonoma)

others
Meursault — France (Côte de Beaune)
Pouilly-Fuissé — France (Burgundy)
White Burgundy (Premier Cru, Grand Cru) — France

hot & creamy crab tartlets

Laura Northey, a participant in my wine course at Fleming College, brought the tuna version of this dip to our last class of the season. Both the tuna and crab versions have been a hit among my friends. Laura obtained the original tuna version of this recipe from one of her favorite cookbooks, The Best of Bridge Cookbook: Royal Treats for Entertaining. *This is my rendition, made into tartlets.*

Serves 4–6 (makes 24 tartlets)

1 lb	500 g	cream cheese, at room temperature (two 8 oz/250 g packages)
2		7 oz (184 g) tins crabmeat
2		green onions, finely chopped
1 tsp	5 mL	horseradish
2 Tbsp	25 mL	sour cream
		sea salt to taste
		freshly ground black pepper to taste
1 Tbsp	15 mL	freshly squeezed lemon juice
2		sheets puff pastry
½ cup	125 mL	slivered almonds

Preheat the oven to 350°F (180°C). Combine all the ingredients, except the puff pastry and almonds, in a medium bowl. Roll out the puff pastry on a lightly floured, clean work surface. Cut out 24 rounds using a 2-inch (5 cm) cookie cutter or the rim of a wine glass. Spray 2 muffin tins with nonstick cooking spray.

Place a pastry round in the bottom of each cup. Drop 1 Tbsp (15 mL) of the crab mixture into each cup. Repeat for all 24 cups. Sprinkle each cup with the slivered almonds. Bake the tartlets for 10 to 15 minutes, until the dough is golden and the crab is heated through. Place them on a platter and serve them warm.

building blocks
The predominant building block is fattiness, due to the cream cheese. A big, fat white has enough fattiness to match.

flavors
Choose a big, fat white with toasty aromas and creamy texture to match the flavor of toasted almonds and the creaminess of the filling.

leftover wine

What do you do with leftover wine? How do you keep it fresh once the bottle is opened? A wine's style helps to determine its life span in an opened bottle. Champagne and sparkling wine have the shortest life span. Inferior sparkling wines will lose their effervescence quickly, so drink them to the last drop once the bottle is opened. If produced in the traditional style known as *méthode champenoise*, sparkling wine and champagne can last a couple of days in the refrigerator, if recorked.

White table wines have a relatively short life span, as well. When recorked and refrigerated, a white wine will stay fresh for a couple of days. It will still be drinkable, but may lose some of its wonderful aromas and flavors. Some white wines with excellent acidity, such as white Burgundy, can retain their character over a few days. Dessert wines, because they're generally high in alcohol and sugar, keep longer when recorked and refrigerated, sometimes for weeks.

Red wines have a love/hate relationship with oxygen. While older vintages are decanted to remove sediment, young reds are decanted to expose them to oxygen so they can breathe. Decanting allows the wine's aromas and flavors to open up. However, if exposed to oxygen for a few days without being recorked and refrigerated, the wine will soon oxidize and eventually turn to vinegar.

If you intend to store an opened bottle of white or red wine overnight, recork the bottle and put it in the refrigerator, standing it upright. Chilling the wine helps slow the oxidation process. I do this regularly, as I often open a bottle to sample the wine, in hopes of drinking a glass at a later time. If I'm refrigerating a half-bottle of quality wine, I'll add a splash of vegetable oil to the bottle. The oil film helps keep the wine from air exposure left inside the bottle, even after recorking. The little oil used doesn't affect the wine at all. It's virtually unnoticeable.

If you want to prolong the life span of your wine for up to a week, consider investing in a vacuum pump. This gadget pumps out air before you recork the bottle. You can purchase pumps such as the VacuVin. To use these devices, you attach the rubber stopper to the bottle's rim. You attach the vacuum to the top of the rubber stopper and suck the air from the bottle.

sex & the lobster sliders

While hosting a client appreciation event at the Estates of Sunnybrook in Toronto, I tried my first grilled lobster sandwich, created by Chef Mike Szabo. I noticed that the majority of the guests were moaning in delight over the rich and buttery lobster flavor of this simple yet sophisticated mini comfort food. Inspired by Chef Mike's recipe, I decided to create my own version for this cookbook.

*Serves 4–6
(makes 6 sliders)*

12 oz	375 g	fresh lobster meat, cut into ½-inch (1 cm) chunks*
½ cup	125 mL	mayonnaise
½ cup	125 mL	finely chopped celery
½ tsp	2 mL	freshly squeezed lemon juice
1 Tbsp	15 mL	finely chopped fresh tarragon
		sea salt to taste
		white pepper to taste
12		slices whole wheat bread
		butter (as needed)

*If you can't find fresh lobster meat, a canned or frozen version will suffice.

Preheat the oven to 350°F (180°C). Combine all the ingredients except the bread and butter in a medium bowl and mix them together well. Cut 12 circles from the bread, using a 3-inch (7.5 cm) cookie cutter. Spoon 1 Tbsp (15 mL) of lobster salad onto each circle. Place another circle on top of it. Coat 1 side of the bread with butter. Place the mini sandwich, butter side down, on a rimmed baking sheet sprayed with nonstick cooking spray. Butter the tops. Repeat, making 6 sandwiches. Bake the sandwiches for about 20 minutes, turning them once, until the sides are golden and the lobster salad is heated through.

building blocks
The predominant building block is fattiness from the lobster, mayonnaise and butter. A big, fat white is the only wine with enough fattiness to match.

flavors
Choose a big, fat white with buttery tones to harmonize with the caramelized butter on these mini sandwiches.

mini battered fish with lemon chive tartar sauce

The classic combination of fish and chips is considered comfort food because it's salty, crispy and fatty. This mini version of fried fish has been spiced up to pair well with wine. You can always add a few pesto fries to the newspaper cone, as well. (See page 102.)

Serves 4–6 (makes 12 pieces of fish)

Tartar sauce:

½ cup	125 mL	mayonnaise
2 Tbsp	25 mL	finely chopped fresh chives
2 Tbsp	25 mL	finely chopped cucumber
1 tsp	5 mL	freshly squeezed lemon juice
1 tsp	5 mL	lemon zest
		sea salt to taste
		freshly ground black pepper to taste

Fish:

2½ lb	1.25 kg	cod fillets, skinned, pin bones removed
		all-purpose flour (for dredging)
		corn oil (for frying)
2 cups	500 mL	all-purpose flour
1 tsp	5 mL	baking powder
pinch		sea salt
1		bottle ale (12 oz/360 mL), ice cold
		newspaper to serve in

Combine all the tartar sauce ingredients in a medium bowl. Cover it and refrigerate it until it's needed.

Cut the fish diagonally into 12 pieces, each about 2 inches (5 cm) long and ½ inch (1 cm) thick. Pat them dry. Dredge them in flour. Let them rest on paper towel.

Fill a deep-fryer with the oil and heat it to 375°F (190°C). Cut the newspaper pages into rectangles about 3 x 6 inches (7.5 x 15 cm). Roll up each rectangle into a cone. Using a stapler, fold over the pointed end of the cone and staple it. Repeat, making 12 cones. Set them aside.

Combine the flour, baking powder and salt in a bowl. Add the ale slowly, until the batter is smooth and not too thick. (You won't need the whole bottle of ale.)

continued on next page

Dip the fish into the batter and then drop it into the hot oil. Fry the fish in batches. Turn it frequently, until it's golden, about 2 to 3 minutes. Transfer it to a paper towel–lined baking sheet and keep it warm in the lower third of the oven.

Season the fish with salt, then put it into the mini cone. Add a dollop of tartar sauce on top. Repeat this process for all 12 cones. Serve the fish hot.

building blocks
The predominant building block is fattiness from the oil and mayonnaise. A big, fat white is a perfect match.

flavors
Choose a big, fat white with citrus flavors to draw out the delicate lemon flavor in the tartar sauce.

mini welsh rarebit

This is a classic comfort food turned into an appetizer.

Serves 4–6 (makes 12 squares)

12		pumpernickel squares or rounds
2 cups	500 mL	grated extra-old cheddar cheese
½ cup	125 mL	freshly grated Parmigiano-Reggiano
⅓ cup	75 mL	ale
3 Tbsp	40 mL	butter
2 Tbsp	25 mL	Dijon mustard
1 cup	250 mL	dried breadcrumbs

Preheat the broiler. Meanwhile, toast the pumpernickel squares. Set them aside. Spray a rimmed baking sheet with nonstick cooking spray. Arrange the squares on the sheet so their sides touch. Combine the cheeses, ale, butter and mustard in a skillet over medium heat. Simmer the sauce on low until it's melted and smooth. Remove it from the heat. Stir in the breadcrumbs. Spoon the mixture over the pumpernickel squares. Broil them until the topping just begins to brown. Remove the baking sheet from the oven immediately. Using a sharp knife, cut between the squares. Transfer the squares to individual platters and serve them hot with chutney.

building blocks
The predominant building block is fattiness due to the cheeses. A big, fat white is the best match.

flavors
Choose a big, fat white with toasty and vanilla tones to harmonize with the Parmigiano and cheddar cheese.

pesto fries

I tried pesto fries for the first time while touring wineries in Napa Valley. They are so yummy, especially with a big, fat Chardonnay. Presented in small cones, they make for a great comfort food appetizer. These fries can also be served in a newspaper cone with the Mini Battered Fish (See page 99.)

Serves 4–6 (makes 12 cones)

1½ lb	750 g	russet potatoes*
1		newspaper
1 cup	250 mL	pesto
		vegetable oil (for deep-frying)

*If in a rush, use frozen fries.

Fill a bowl with water and add ice. Cut the potatoes into ⅛-inch-thick (3 mm) fries. Place the raw potatoes in the cold water. Refrigerate them for 30 minutes. Cut the newspaper pages into rectangles, about 3 x 6 inches (7.5 x 15 cm). Roll up each rectangle into a cone, with an opening about 2 inches (5 cm) in diameter and a pointed end. Using a stapler, fold over the pointed end of the cone and staple it. Repeat, making 12 cones. Set them aside.

Heat the pesto in a large saucepan over medium heat. Reduce the heat to low and simmer the pesto until it's needed.

Fill a large, deep pot or deep-fryer with the oil and heat it to 375°F (190°C). Remove the potatoes from the fridge and drain them. Pat the potatoes dry. Deep-fry them until they're golden, about 3 to 4 minutes. Remove the fries from the oil using a slotted spoon. Toss the fries in the hot pesto. Heap a handful of pesto fries into each cone. Serve them hot.

building blocks
The predominant building block is fattiness due to the deep-fried potatoes and pesto. A big, fat white is the ideal match.

flavors
Choose a big, fat white with toasty flavor to complement the flavor of the pesto.

noninterventionist wine-making

There's a new buzz phrase called "noninterventionist wine-making." A growing number of small wine producers, especially in California, are embracing this philosophy.

"Noninterventionist" means the winemaker interferes as little as possible with the growing of the grapes and the production of the wine.

To date, no defined rules or governing body regulates this wine-making approach, so noninterventionists can practice a variety of wine-making methods. Some of these include the use of wild yeast strains to ferment wine.

Thousands of wild yeast strains exist in the air and cling to grapes and other surfaces in the vineyard and winery. The noninterventionist does not interfere, but rather allows the fermentation process to occur naturally. A strain of wild yeast comes into contact with the natural sugars in the picked grapes and a spontaneous fermentation begins.

Spontaneous fermentation is considered a risky business, as not all wild yeasts produce sufficient alcohol levels. For many noninterventionists, it's worth the risk to allow this natural process to take place, because they believe it produces distinctive, superior wine. Still, making wine with wild yeast has been a source of debate for many because of its unpredictable nature.

For the last century, most winemakers have been using cultured yeast strains as they produce consistent and predictable results in less time than wild yeast requires. Many cultured yeast strains exist, each enhancing different characteristics in the wine, such as the aromas or mouthfeel. The winemaker's job includes researching and experimenting with different yeasts, eventually discovering the ones best suited to certain grape varieties and wines.

With this method, sulfur dioxide (SO_2) is added to the grape must (crushed grapes and juice) to stun or kill wild yeasts and inhibit the growth of spoilage organisms. The cultured yeast strain is added to the must to launch the fermentation.

Noninterventionists can use other techniques, as well, such as a minimal racking of the wine and a gravity flow system.

Racking is part of the clarification process by which wine is cleared of dead yeast cells and particles after fermentation. Some noninterventionists rack as little as possible, believing the process strips wine of its distinctiveness and character.

A gravity flow winery is usually built into a hillside or mountain on various levels, sometimes having as many as seven tiers. After harvesting, the grapes are brought to the highest level of the winery. Depending on the number of tiers, different wine-making processes can take place on each level. This gravity flow allows the grapes, juice and wine to flow naturally downward. The noninterventionist believes pumping bruises both the grapes and the resulting wine.

fried green tomatoes & fried zucchini

My husband, Jack, is not a zucchini fan. I made a tray of this appetizer and asked him to "sample" it. I figured that if Jack liked it, this easy recipe could be worth trying on guests. He ate the entire platter, all 24 pieces!

Serves 4–6 (makes about 24 tomatoes and zucchini)

Dipping sauce:

1		bulb garlic
⅔ cup	150 mL	pine nuts
3 Tbsp	40 mL	olive oil
1 Tbsp	15 mL	freshly squeezed lemon juice
¼ cup	50 mL	water (more if needed)
1 Tbsp	15 mL	finely chopped fresh parsley
		sea salt to taste
		freshly ground black pepper to taste

Vegetables:

½ lb	250 g	baby zucchinis, washed
½ lb	250 g	green tomatoes
3 Tbsp	40 mL	all-purpose flour
1 tsp	5 mL	paprika
½ tsp	2 mL	sea salt
½ tsp	2 mL	freshly ground black pepper
1		egg, lightly beaten
		vegetable oil (for frying)

Preheat the oven to 350°F (180°C). To make the sauce, bake the garlic bulb for 45 minutes or until its skin turns black. Remove it and let it cool. Open the end of each garlic clove with a sharp knife, squeeze the cloves out of their papery skins and add the cloves to the bowl of a food processor or blender. Add the pine nuts, olive oil, lemon juice and water. Purée the mixture until it's smooth. Add more water, if needed, to turn the mixture into a sauce. Fold in the parsley. Season the mixture with salt and pepper. Transfer it to a bowl suitable for dips. Cover it and refrigerate it until it's needed.

Cut the zucchini on a diagonal, about ¼ inch (5 mm) thick. Slice the tomatoes about ¼ inch (5 mm) thick. Combine the flour, paprika, salt and pepper in a bowl. Heat the oil over medium heat in a skillet. Put the zucchini and tomato slices into the bowl with the flour mixture and toss the vegetables in the mixture. Shake off the excess flour.

Dip each slice into the beaten egg and place as many as you can, without crowding, in the skillet. Fry the zucchini and tomato slices in batches until they're golden, about 30 seconds per side. Remove them with a fork. Place them on paper towel. Serve the hot zucchini and tomato slices with the sauce.

building blocks
The predominant building block is fattiness, due to the frying and the oil in pine nuts. A big, fat white is perfect.

flavors
Choose a big, fat white with toasty notes to complement the nutty flavor of the pine nuts.

mini cilantro whole wheat pancakes with avocado tapenade

I love this simple, tasty appetizer. The ingredients are inexpensive and it's supereasy to make. It's a great party-starter when you know your guests are consuming high-alcohol wines. The fattiness of the dish helps to absorb some of the alcohol.

For 4–6 (makes 16 pancakes)

Pancakes:

1 cup	250 mL	whole wheat flour
½ tsp	2 mL	baking powder
1		egg, lightly beaten
½ cup	125 mL	milk
2 Tbsp	25 mL	finely chopped fresh cilantro
		freshly ground black pepper

Tapenade:

½		ripe avocado, finely chopped
¼ cup	50 mL	butter, softened
1 Tbsp	15 mL	freshly squeezed lime juice
		freshly ground black pepper to taste
		sour cream (for garnish)
		cilantro leaves, finely chopped (for garnish)

Sift together the flour and the baking powder in a medium bowl. Make a well in the center. Add the egg and the milk. Whisk the batter until it's smooth. Fold in the cilantro. Season it with the pepper.

Spray the inside of a large skillet with nonstick cooking spray and place it over medium heat. Drop 1 Tbsp (15 mL) of batter into the skillet using a spoon. Cook the pancakes, in batches, until the edges bubble on the first side. Flip them and cook the other side until the pancakes are lightly golden. Remove them and set them on paper towel. Repeat until all the batter is used up. Keep the pancakes warm.

Combine all the tapenade ingredients in a bowl. Mix them together until they form a smooth paste. Spread the pancakes with tapenade. Garnish each pancake with a small dollop of sour cream, sprinkle each with fresh cilantro and arrange them all on a platter. Serve them at room temperature.

building blocks
The predominant building block is fattiness, due to the avocado. A big, fat white wine is the ideal partner.

flavors
Choose a big, fat white with herbal tones to bring out the delicate flavor of the cilantro.

bacon-cheddar melt

An addiction is a recurring compulsion by an individual to engage in some specific activity. What could be more addictive than a dip loaded with umami-rich cheese and bacon? I am a member of a local home wine-making group, and member Susan Lunn brought this dip to our picnic. All of us seemed to have a recurring compulsion to engage in the specific activity of dipping into this bacon-cheddar melt. The melt vanished not long after it was served, leaving the other appetizers look-ing very lonely. Susan was generous enough to share her orgasmic recipe with me.

Serves 4–6

1 lb	500 g	bacon
1 lb	500 g	sliced mushrooms
1		onion, finely chopped
¾ cup	175 mL	sour cream
2 tsp	10 mL	freshly squeezed lemon juice
3 Tbsp	40 mL	all-purpose flour
2 cups	500 mL	shredded extra-old cheddar cheese
		baguette

Preheat the oven to 350°F (180°C). Fry the bacon until it's crisp, about 10 minutes, in a large skillet over medium heat. Remove it from the skillet and drain it on paper towel. Crumble the bacon into small pieces. Set it aside.

Drain most of the fat from the skillet. Sauté the mushrooms and onion in the remaining fat over medium heat until they're tender, 7 to 10 minutes. Transfer the bacon, mushrooms and onion to a bowl. Add the sour cream, lemon juice and flour. Mix them well. Pour the mixture into a 4-cup (1 L) glass baking dish. Top it with the shredded cheese. Bake it for 20 minutes, until the cheese is melted. Serve the "melt" hot in the baking dish with slices of baguette.

building blocks
The predominant building block is fattiness, due to the bacon and cheddar cheese. A big, fat white has enough fattiness to match.

flavors
Choose a big, fat white with smoky tones to harmonize with the flavor of the bacon.

chilled spinach & three-cheese dip

Here's a good ol' reliable to offset the gourmet appetizers you'll be serving. It's always smart to offer at least two oldies for the conservatives.

Serves 4–6

8 oz	250 g	cream cheese, softened
½ cup	125 mL	mayonnaise
⅓ cup	75 mL	chopped green onions
1		package frozen chopped spinach (10 oz/300 g), thawed and well drained
½ cup	125 mL	freshly grated Parmigiano-Reggiano
½ cup	125 mL	shredded Monterey Jack
½ cup	125 mL	chopped red bell peppers
		tortilla chips or chunks of baguette

Combine the cream cheese, mayonnaise and half the onions in a medium bowl. Beat the mixture with an electric mixer until it's well blended. Add the spinach, mixing it in by hand until it's just blended. Fold in the cheeses and peppers. Cover the dip and refrigerate it for at least 1 hour. Sprinkle it with the remaining green onion. Serve it cold with tortilla chips or chunks of baguette.

building blocks
The predominant building block is fattiness, due to the cream cheese, mayonnaise and cheeses. A big, fat white wine is perfect.

flavors
Choose a big, fat white with smoky flavor to complement the flavors of the cheese.

scallop & parmesan pouches

Talk about a recipe celebrating the fifth taste sensation! Scallops, Parmigiano-Reggiano and Worcestershire sauce are all umami-rich. No wonder this recipe provides the MOAN FACTOR.

Serves 4–6 (makes 30 pouches)

30		slices of whole wheat bread (4 x 4 inches/ 10 x 10 cm)
2 Tbsp	25 mL	butter
2		cloves fresh garlic, minced
½ tsp	2 mL	freshly squeezed lemon juice
1 tsp	5 mL	finely chopped fresh dill
1 cup	250 mL	chopped fresh scallops
dash		Worcestershire sauce
		sea salt to taste
		freshly ground black pepper to taste
½ cup	125 mL	freshly grated Parmigiano-Reggiano
1		egg beaten with 1 tsp (5 mL) water
		corn oil (for frying)

Cut 2 rounds from each slice of bread with a 2-inch (5 cm) cookie cutter, making 60 rounds. Melt the butter in a skillet over medium heat. Add the garlic and sauté it until it's aromatic. Add the lemon, dill, scallops and Worcestershire sauce. Sauté the mixture until the scallops are done, about 2 minutes. Do not overcook. Remove the scallop mixture from the heat and transfer it into a bowl. Season it to taste with salt and pepper. Fold in the Parmigiano.

Place about 1 tsp (5 mL) of the scallop mixture in the center of a bread circle. Using your finger, spread the egg wash around the perimeter of the circle. Cover it with another circle. Press the edges of the circles together, using a fork. Repeat, making 30 pouches. Heat the oil in a large skillet. Fry the pouches until they're golden. Place them on a platter and serve them hot.

building blocks
The predominant building block is fattiness from the rich scallops, Parmigiano and oil. A big, fat white has enough fattiness to match.

flavors
Choose a big, fat white with some citrus tones to draw forth the delicate flavor of lemon in these pouches.

meatballs in camembert sauce

The bouillon cube goes a long way in adding depth of flavor to the sauce for these meatballs. Bouillon cubes are condensed umami.

Serves 4–6 (makes 26–30 meatballs)

2 Tbsp	25 mL	butter
¼ cup	50 mL	finely chopped onion
2 lb	1 kg	ground pork
⅓ cup	75 mL	milk
⅓ cup	75 mL	dried breadcrumbs
2		eggs, lightly beaten
2 Tbsp	25 mL	all-purpose flour
¾ cup	175 mL	water
½ cup	125 mL	white wine
1		chicken bouillon cube
2 oz	60 g	Camembert cheese, rind removed
		freshly ground black pepper to taste
		toothpicks

Preheat the oven to 425°F (220°C). Melt the butter in a small skillet over medium heat. Add the onion and sauté it until it's golden, about 4 minutes. Transfer the onion to a bowl, reserving the butter in the saucepan. Add to the onion the pork, milk, breadcrumbs and eggs. Mix them together until they're well blended.

Shape the mixture into 1-inch (2.5 cm) balls. Set the meatballs on a rimmed baking sheet sprayed with nonstick cooking spray. Bake them, turning as needed, until all their sides are golden, about 15 to 20 minutes in total. Transfer the meatballs to a serving platter.

To make the sauce, stir the flour into the butter in the skillet. Cook the butter/flour over medium heat, stirring, until it's bubbly. Remove it from the heat. Add the water and the wine. Add the bouillon cube and let it dissolve. Mix the sauce well. Heat the sauce again, stirring. Add the cheese. Stir the mixture until the cheese melts and the sauce thickens. Season it with pepper. Pour the sauce over the meatballs. Serve the meatballs hot, on a platter, with toothpicks.

building blocks
The predominant building block is fattiness from the sauce. A big, fat white is a perfect match.

flavors
Choose a big, fat white with yeasty character to match the flavor of the Camembert.

orgasmic appetizers to pair with off-dry whites

Off-dry whites

PREDOMINANT BUILDING BLOCKS:
Balance of sourness and fruitiness with some sweetness.

FLAVORS:
Tropical citrus and hard fruits; floral notes, such as roses; minerals, nutty and spicy tones.

WINES PRODUCED IN THE OFF-DRY WHITE STYLE

- Wines produced in this style are often perceived as suited to wine novices because of their sweetness level. But off-dry white wines have an important place at the table. This level of sweetness is the ideal building block that perfectly offsets, and therefore harmonizes with, hot and spicy ethnic cuisine.

- Off-dry whites, due to their sweetness, are medium- to full-bodied.

- Wine lovers who detest wines with sweetness discover a new appreciation for them when they're properly paired with food. It's worth opening your mind and trying these new combinations. The appetizer course is a good place to start.

- The sweetness in these wines comes from a few sources. The winemaker may halt the fermentation before all the grape's natural sugars have been transformed to alcohol and carbon dioxide, leaving a level of natural sweetness in the resulting wines.

- The winemaker may also "vinify" the wine dry, which means fermenting the wine until all the sugar has been transformed into alcohol and carbon dioxide. Then, natural grape juice is added back into the wine to produce a level of sweetness.

- Sweetness is left in a resulting wine in an effort to balance its acidity, so a quality wine produced in this style will not be overly sweet.

- Best food matches include vegetables with natural sweetness like squash and sweet potatoes, slow-roasted beets and slow-roasted carrots.

- Hot and spicy foods with light to medium heat sing alongside wines produced in this style.

The regions below are stylistically noted for producing off-dry whites.

REGIONS

riesling
Canada (British Columbia, Ontario)
Germany

gewürztraminer
Canada (British Columbia, Ontario)
France (Alsace)
Germany

colombard
Australia
United States (California)

others
Sylvaner — France (Alsace)
Müller-Thurgau — Germany

mini grilled cheese with black pepper & a dollop of banana ketchup

My brother Jay loves to cook as much as I do. While visiting, Jay made me his "house special"—Jay's famous grilled cheese sandwich with banana ketchup. I told him I would only take a few bites. I was dieting and didn't want the extra fat. I dipped this grilled cheese into the banana ketchup, took a bite and swore I'd gone to heaven. I ended up eating two grilled cheese sandwiches as we sat together and watched a series of cooking shows on the Food Channel. I've converted his recipe into appetizer-sized sandwiches. Your guests will love these babies. There's nothing like comfort food, mini-sized, to feed the soul. You may want to double the recipe, just in case.

Serves 4–6 (makes 6 mini sandwiches)

12		slices of sourdough bread (¼ inch/5 mm thick)
12		slices of extra-old cheddar cheese (⅛ inch /3 mm thick)
		freshly ground black pepper
		butter (as needed)
¾ cup	175 mL	grated Asiago cheese
3		slices of maple cured bacon
		banana ketchup (facing page)

Cut 12 circles from the bread using a 3-inch (7.5 cm) cookie cutter. Place 1 slice of cheddar cheese on 6 of the rounds. Season it with black pepper. Place the other rounds on top. Trim the cheese from the edges. Butter the top rounds. Sprinkle the buttered rounds with the Asiago cheese. Pat the cheese into the butter. Turn the sandwiches over and butter the other side. Sprinkle this buttered side with Asiago. Pat the cheese into the butter. In a large skillet over medium heat, fry the bacon until crisp. Remove the bacon and reserve it for another sandwich. Remove half the bacon fat from the skillet; reserve it.

Lower the heat to medium. Fry the sandwiches until they're golden on 1 side, about 2 minutes. Add more bacon fat and fry the other side of the sandwiches until they're golden, about 2 minutes. Top them with a dollop of banana ketchup and arrange the sandwiches on a platter. Serve them hot.

Banana ketchup:

1 Tbsp	15 mL	vegetable oil
¼ cup	50 mL	finely chopped onions
1 tsp	5 mL	finely chopped fresh ginger
2		cloves garlic, minced
2		mangoes, peeled and diced
2		bananas, peeled and sliced
pinch		ground cloves
pinch		nutmeg
pinch		allspice
2 Tbsp	25 mL	maple syrup
2 Tbsp	25 mL	white balsamic vinegar
1 Tbsp	15 mL	finely chopped fresh cilantro
		water (as needed)
¼ cup	50 mL	freshly squeezed lime juice
		sea salt to taste

Heat the oil in a large skillet over medium heat. Sauté the onions, ginger and garlic until they're soft. Add the remaining ingredients, except for the lime juice and salt. Turn down the heat and simmer the mixture over low heat, stirring frequently, for 15 to 20 minutes. Remove it from the heat. Let it cool. Purée the ketchup in a food processor or blender until it's smooth, adding water to thin it, if necessary. Add the lime juice and salt. Serve at room temperature.

building blocks
The primary building blocks are fattiness from the cheeses and sweetness in the ketchup. An off-dry white has enough weight and sweetness to match.

flavors
Choose an off-dry white with tropical flavors to harmonize with the ketchup.

sequoia grill wok squid

While working in Vancouver, I dined with four women at the Sequoia Grill at the Teahouse in Stanley Park, Vancouver. We shared the Wok Squid appetizer, pairing it with an off-dry white wine. All four of us moaned in delight. I asked to speak with Chef Michael Knowlson. Chef Michael is a generous soul and willingly gave me this recipe to share with you. He is part of a new breed of European chefs who have crossed the Atlantic in search of challenging new environments and ingredients indigenous to Canada's West Coast.

Serves 4–6

3 cups	750 mL	fresh or frozen squid (tubes only)
2		eggs
		cornstarch (as needed)
¼ cup	50 mL	minced white onion
1		jalapeño pepper, cored and minced
½ tsp	2 mL	Vietnamese garlic chili paste*
		peanut oil (for deep-frying)
1 Tbsp	15 mL	sesame oil
2 tsp	10 mL	white sesame seeds
2 Tbsp	25 mL	black sesame seeds
		sea salt to taste
		green onions (for garnish)
1		English cucumber, sliced (for garnish)

*You can substitute Chinese garlic chili paste; it's available at Asian supermarkets and most grocery stores.

Butterfly the squid tubes to open them, lay them flat and scrape them inside to get them clean. Score the inside edges with diagonal cuts. Slice the squid into strips about ½ x 1½ inches (1 x 4 cm). Whisk the eggs with equal parts water; toss the squid with the mixture. Toss the squid in cornstarch to coat it.

Mix together the minced onion, jalapeño and chili sauce. Fill a large, deep pot or deep-fryer with oil. Let the oil heat to 365°F (185°C). Fry the squid for about 2 minutes or until lightly golden. Drain it on paper towel.

In a small skillet over medium heat, mix the chili mixture with the sesame oil. Sauté it for 2 minutes or until it's heated through. Add the cooked squid and toss it in the chili mixture. Add the sesame seeds and a little salt and toss. Heap the warm squid on a platter and sprinkle it with the green onion and cucumber.

building blocks
The predominant building block is heat and spice due to the chili paste. An off-dry white has the sweetness to offset the heat and spice.

flavors
Choose an off-dry white with citrus flavors to harmonize with the flavor of the squid.

sweet jerk skewers

If you love salt, fat, heat and spice, this recipe will cause a culinary orgasm for you. My friend, the talented chef David Franklin, made this appetizer for my friends and me, using my Sweet Jerk dry rub.

Serves 4–6 (6 skewers)

1 lb	500 g	mild pancetta, not sliced
2 Tbsp	25 mL	honey, heated
½ cup	125 mL	Orgasmic Culinary Creations Sweet Jerk dry rub*
6		bamboo skewers (6 inch/15 cm), soaked overnight in water (soak some extras just in case; they're cheap)
18		cubes of fresh pineapple

*Turn to the last page for more details on how to purchase Sweet Jerk. Or substitute with homemade Jamaican Seasoning (page 219).

Unroll the pancetta along its natural seam and square off the edges. Level the slab with a sharp knife so the end is reasonably even. Cut it into eighteen ¾-inch (2 cm) cubes. Fill a medium-sized pot with water and bring it to a boil, then drop the cubes into the pot and boil them for 1½ minutes. Drain them and while they're still warm, place the cubes in a mixing bowl. Toss them with half the honey and half the Sweet Jerk. Allow them to cool on a baking tray.

Toss the pineapple cubes in a bowl with the rest of the honey and Sweet Jerk. Set them aside. Preheat a gas or charcoal grill. Thread each skewer with a cube of pancetta and then a cube of pineapple. Repeat 2 more times. Each skewer should have 3 cubes of pancetta and 3 cubes of pineapple. Grill the 6 skewers over medium-high heat for about 1½ minutes per side and then move them to a cooler part of the grill to heat through. Transfer them to a platter and serve them hot.

building blocks

The predominant building blocks are saltiness from the pancetta, sweetness from the pineapple and heat and spice from the Sweet Jerk. An off-dry white has enough sourness to offset the saltiness and enough sweetness to offset the heat and spice. The wine's sweetness also complements the coconut.

flavors

Choose an off-dry white with tropical flavors to complement the flavor of the pineapple.

sweet jerk beer-battered shrimp with marmalade dipping sauce

This is my version of a well-known recipe called coconut beer-battered shrimp. If you decide to add more heat and spice, be sure to choose a wine with sufficient sweetness to match.

Serves 4–6 (makes 24 shrimp)

		corn oil (for deep-frying)
1		egg, lightly beaten
½ cup	125 mL	all-purpose flour (divided in half)
⅔ cup	150 mL	beer
1½ tsp	7 mL	baking powder
¼ cup	50 mL	all-purpose flour
¼ cup	50 mL	Orgasmic Culinary Creations Sweet Jerk dry rub*
24		large raw shrimp, peeled (keep the tails on)
		Marmalade Dipping Sauce (page 61)

*Turn to the last page for more details on how to purchase Sweet Jerk. Or substitute it with homemade Jamaican Seasoning (see page 219).

Fill a deep-fryer or deep skillet with enough oil for deep-frying. Heat the oil over high heat to 350°F (180°C). Combine the egg, ¼ cup (50 mL) of the flour, the beer and the baking powder in a medium bowl to make a batter, not too thick and not too thin. Pour the remaining flour into another bowl and pour ¼ cup (50 mL) of Sweet Jerk dry rub into a third bowl.

Hold the shrimp by their tails and dredge them in flour. Shake off the excess flour. Dip them in the batter, allowing the excess to drip off. Roll the shrimp in Sweet Jerk. Place the coated shrimp on a rimmed baking sheet lined with wax paper. Cover them and refrigerate them for 30 minutes.

Deep-fry the shrimp in batches for 2 to 3 minutes or until they're golden. Using tongs, carefully remove the shrimp and drain them on paper towel. Arrange them on a platter and serve them warm with Marmalade Dipping Sauce.

building blocks
The predominant building blocks are heat and spice from the Sweet Jerk and sweetness from the coconut and dipping sauce. An off-dry white has enough sweetness to offset the heat and spice and harmonize with the coconut and the dipping sauce.

flavors
Choose an off-dry white with tropical flavors to harmonize with the coconut in the Sweet Jerk.

seared scallop with a pickled ginger & clementine butter sauce

In 2006 and 2007 I had the blessing of working with Chef Andy Chong of the Vancouver Golf Club. Before joining the golf club, Chef Andy worked at one of Vancouver's most acclaimed restaurants, CinCin. He apprenticed under Chef Brad Thompson. In October of 2005 he moved to the Vancouver Golf Club to satisfy two of his passions, cooking and golf. In Tofino on Vancouver Island, Chef Andy once served this appetizer to the late Charlton Heston, who was blown away by the flavors. It now makes up 20 percent of his appetizer sales at the Vancouver Golf Club.

Serves 4–6 (makes 8 scallops)

4		clementine oranges
1 Tbsp	15 mL	canola oil
½ cup	125 mL	salted butter
8		large scallops
½ cup	125 mL	off-dry white wine
		sea salt to taste
		freshly ground black pepper to taste
2 Tbsp	25 mL	juice from the pickled ginger
½ tsp	2 mL	wasabi paste*
8		slices pickled ginger*

*Pickled ginger and wasabi paste are available at Asian supermarkets.

Zest 1 of the clementines into a small bowl. Save it for juicing. Peel and segment 2 of the 4 clementines, removing their membranes. You need 8 nice segments. Set them aside. Juice the remaining 2 clementines.

In a thick-bottomed skillet, heat the oil and 2 Tbsp (25 mL) of the butter. Season the scallops with salt and pepper, add to the skillet and sear on 1 side, about 90 seconds. Sear the other side, about 1 minute. Remove the scallops from the skillet using a slotted spoon. Let any residual fat fall back into the skillet. Set the scallops on a plate.

Place the skillet back on the burner and deglaze with the white wine. Reduce it until 2 Tbsp (25 mL) remains. Add the clementine juice, zest, pickled ginger juice and wasabi and simmer, reducing the liquid until there's about ¼ cup (50 mL) left. Whisk in the remainder of the butter, then add the ginger. Fold in the clementine segments, stirring until they're warm. Return the scallops to the pan to coat with sauce and reheat. Serve scallops on individual Chinese soup spoons, drizzled with sauce and topped with a clementine wedge.

building blocks
The predominant building block is sweetness from the clementines. An off-dry white has enough sweetness to match.

flavors
Choose an off-dry white with citrus tones to harmonize with the flavor of the clementines.

mandarin pancakes with peking duck

I first tasted a version of this recipe in the early 1990s. Michelle Ramsay, who cowrote Canada's Wine Country Cookbook with me, made these jewels for our book launch party. I've been making my version of them ever since. This appetizer is always a big hit. Thanks, Michelle!

*Serves 4–6
(makes 12 pancakes)*

3		green onions
3		medium carrots, peeled
3		celery stalks
1		cooked duck (5 lb/2.67 kg)
1 lb	500 g	all-purpose flour
1 cup	250 mL	boiling water (more if needed)
1 tsp	5 mL	sesame oil
		toasted sesame oil (as needed)
		hoisin (as needed)

Cut the white parts off the green onions and reserve them. Slice the green onions into thin vertical strips, about 4 strips per onion. The strips should be about 8 inches (20 cm) long. Cut the carrots and celery into 12 thin vertical strips about 6 inches (15 cm) long.

Remove the skin and the fat layer from the duck. Scrape the fat from the skin, reserve it and cut the skin into 12 thin strips, about 4 inches (10 cm) long. Fry the skin until it's crispy in a skillet over medium heat. Remove and drain on paper towel, and let cool. Cut the duck meat into 12 thin strips, about 4 inches (10 cm) long.

To make the pancakes, sift the flour into a bowl. Add the boiling water and sesame oil. Knead the mixture into a firm dough. Divide the dough into 3 evenly sized balls on a lightly floured clean work surface. Divide each of the balls into 4 mini balls, flattening each into a 4-inch (10 cm) diameter pancake with a rolling pin. Make 12 pancakes.

Brush 1 side of each of the pancakes with sesame oil. Place 2 pancakes together, with the oil on the inside. Make 6 double pancakes. Roll the doubles together using a rolling pin. Fry the pancakes until brown spots appear in a dry skillet over high heat, and fry the other side until brown spots appear. Remove them from the heat, gently pull them apart, and cover with a damp cloth. Repeat until all the pancakes are cooked. You should have 12 pancakes.

Spread a generous amount of hoisin on each pancake, on the oiled side. Place 1 strip of fat, 1 strip of duck, 1 carrot strip and 1 celery strip in the middle of each pancake. Roll it up and tie it with the green onion strip. Repeat. Arrange the pancakes on a platter and serve them at room temperature.

building blocks
The predominant building block is sweetness from the hoisin. An off-dry white has enough sweetness to match the sweetness of the hoisin.

flavors
Choose an off-dry white with tropical flavors to pair nicely with the flavor of the hoisin.

chipotle goat cheese dip with bagel wedges

This is a great dip for nontasters, who tend to enjoy bold flavors. Be sure to pair the heat of the dip with the sweetness of the wine. The hotter and spicier the dip, the more sweetness you'll need in your off-dry white.

Serves 4–6

1 lb	500 g	fresh goat cheese, at room temperature
8 oz	250 g	cream cheese
2 Tbsp	25 mL	adobo sauce from a can of chipotles
3		cloves garlic, minced
1		jalapeño chili, minced, seeds removed
2		eggs, beaten
		freshly ground black pepper
6		bagels
1 Tbsp	15 mL	finely chopped fresh cilantro (for garnish)

Preheat the oven to 400°F (200°C). Cream the cheeses together in a bowl. Add the adobo sauce, garlic, jalapeño and eggs. Season the mixture with black pepper, mixing it together well. Pour it into an 8-inch square (20 cm) glass baking dish. Smooth its surface. Bake it for 20 to 25 minutes, or until the dip is bubbling.

Meanwhile, toast the bagels. Using a serrated knife, slice each half bagel into 4 wedges. Place them in a breadbasket. Remove the dip from the oven. Sprinkle it with the cilantro. Serve the hot dip with the bagel wedges.

building blocks
The predominant building block is heat and spice due to the chipotle and the jalapeño. An off-dry white has enough sweetness to offset the heat and spice.

flavors
Choose an off-dry white with citrus flavors to harmonize with the tangy flavor of the goat cheese.

chinese sesame-coated pork skewers

This is a fabulous appetizer you can make in advance. With the right wine match, the flavors of the fruit sing!

Serves 4–6 (makes 24 skewers)

½ cup	125 mL	hoisin
1 Tbsp	15 mL	light soy sauce
2 Tbsp	25 mL	rice vinegar
2 Tbsp	25 mL	sesame oil
1 tsp	5 mL	finely chopped fresh ginger
1½ lb	750 g	pork, cut into 48 cubes (1 inch/2.5 cm)
6		ripe mangoes, cut into 48 cubes (1 inch/2.5 cm)
1		pineapple, peeled, sliced and cut into 48 cubes (1 inch/2.5 cm)
		sesame seeds (as needed)
24		bamboo skewers (6 inch/15 cm), soaked overnight in water (soak some extras just in case; they're cheap)

Combine the hoisin, soy sauce, vinegar, oil and ginger in a bowl. Add the pork. Cover the mixture and refrigerate it overnight. Arrange 1 cube of pork, 1 cube of mango and 1 cube of pineapple on a skewer. Repeat so each skewer has 2 cubes of pork, mango and pineapple. Pour the sesame seeds onto a plate. Roll each skewer in sesame seeds so they coat all sides. Set the skewers on a rimmed baking sheet. Cover and refrigerate them until they're needed, no more than 4 hours. Barbecue the skewers on the grill for 8 to 10 minutes, turning them once, until the pork is white. Do not let the pork burn. Arrange the skewers on a platter and serve them hot.

building blocks
The predominant building block is sweetness from the mango and pineapple. An off-dry white has enough sweetness to match.

flavors
Choose an off-dry white with tropical flavors to harmonize with the flavor of the fruit.

roasted beet tempura with lemon mint mayonnaise

This recipe appears to use a lot of ingredients. However, many of them are readily available in your kitchen. This is a delicious appetizer for summer, especially for your vegetarian friends.

Serves 4–6 (makes 24 pieces of tempura)

6–8		medium-sized red and yellow beets

Lemon mint mayonnaise:

1		egg yolk
1 tsp	5 mL	Dijon mustard
2 tsp	10 mL	maple syrup
½ cup	125 mL	olive oil
½ cup	125 mL	canola oil
3		large cloves garlic, minced
1 Tbsp	15 mL	freshly squeezed lemon juice
		sea salt to taste
		freshly ground black pepper (to taste)
¼ cup	50 mL	finely chopped fresh mint
1 tsp	5 mL	lemon zest

Batter:

1 cup	250 mL	all-purpose flour
1 cup	250 mL	cornstarch
2 tsp	10 mL	baking soda
2 tsp	10 mL	sugar
1 tsp	5 mL	salt
2		eggs
1 cup	250 mL	water, more if needed
		corn oil (for deep-frying)
		mint leaves (for garnish)

Preheat the oven to 400°F (200°C). Wash and trim the beets. Place them on a rimmed baking sheet sprayed with nonstick cooking spray. Roast the beets until they're tender, 45 to 60 minutes. Let them cool.

Meanwhile, prepare the mayonnaise. Combine the egg yolk, mustard, maple syrup, oils, garlic and lemon juice in a food processor or blender. Pulse the mixture until it's well blended. Then purée it until it turns into a thick mayonnaise. Transfer it to a bowl. Season with salt and pepper. Fold in the mint and the lemon zest. Cover the mayonnaise and refrigerate it until it's needed, but no more than 2 hours.

Using a paring knife, peel the beets. Cut them into ¼-inch (5 mm) slices.

To make the batter, sift together the dry ingredients. Beat the eggs slightly. Add the eggs to the dry ingredients. Slowly add the water. Stir the batter only until it's mixed; it will be slightly lumpy.

Add enough oil to a large pot or skillet for deep-frying. Let the oil heat to 375°F (190°C). Dip the beet slices into the batter. Fry the beets, flipping them once, until they're golden on both sides, about 30 to 40 seconds per side. Fry them in batches. Drain the beets on paper towel. Arrange the beets on a serving platter with a bowl of mayonnaise alongside. Garnish the tempura with mint.

building blocks
The predominant building blocks are sweetness, due to the beets and mayonnaise and fattiness, due to deep-frying. An off-dry white wine with sweetness harmonizes with the beets and has enough weight to stand up to the fattiness of the batter.

flavors
Choose an off-dry white with some herbal notes to bring out the delicate flavor of mint in the mayonnaise.

tuna spring rolls with fresh herbs & wasabi mayonnaise

*I created this Thai-
and Japanese-inspired
appetizer for my
friend's wedding.
I never expected it to
be the first to vanish
from the appetizer
table. Many guests
asked me for this
recipe. If you're prepar-
ing the spring rolls
right before serving,
one rice paper per roll
will suffice. However,
if you're making them
in advance, double up
on the skins to keep
them from splitting.*

*Serves 4–6
(makes 6 rolls)*

2		6 oz (170 g) cans of tuna
½ cup	125 mL	mayonnaise
1 Tbsp	15 mL	wasabi paste*
2 Tbsp	25 mL	each finely chopped fresh mint, cilantro and basil
		sea salt to taste
		freshly ground black pepper to taste
6		rice paper rounds (6 inch/15 cm in diameter)*
		mixed greens (as needed)
		vegetable oil (as needed)

*Rice paper rounds and wasabi paste are available at Asian super-markets and many supermarkets in general.

Combine the tuna, mayonnaise, wasabi and fresh herbs in a bowl. Season the mixture with salt and pepper. Set it aside.

Pour hot tap water into another bowl. Place 1 rice paper round in the water and let it soak for 15 seconds, until it's soft. Pull the round from the water, letting the excess water drip off. Be careful not to split the rice paper. Place the round on a work surface. Place 1 Tbsp (15 mL) of tuna mixture on each round. Add a small handful of mixed greens to the tuna. Fold the round over the ingredients, then roll the rice paper wrapper into a jellyroll (folding over the sides and ends to ensure the filling stays in). Repeat the process if you're double-wrapping (see left). Coat your serving dish with a fine layer of vegetable oil to keep the rolls from sticking to it. Place a damp cloth over the rolls and refrigerate them until they're ready to serve, but no more than 2 hours.

building blocks
The predominant building blocks are sweetness from the mayon-naise and heat from the wasabi. An off-dry white harmonizes with the mayonnaise and nicely offsets the heat.

flavors
Choose an off-dry white with herbal notes to complement the delicate taste of the fresh herbs.

prosciutto & cantaloupe fingers

Prosciutto with canta-
loupe is certainly a
classic combination of
flavors, qualifying as
a tantric twosome!
Here's a fun and new
way to show off this
dynamic duo.

Serves 4–6
(makes 30 pieces)

1 lb	500 g	cream cheese, at room temperature (two 8 oz/250 g packages)
½ cup	125 mL	finely chopped fresh mint
1		small cantaloupe
½ lb	250 g	prosciutto slices (thinly shaved), about 30 slices
10		slices raisin bread
30		small mint leaves
		piping bag

Combine the cream cheese and mint in a small bowl. Mix them together well. Cut the cantaloupe in half, then in quarters. Remove the seeds. Peel the quarters. Cut the quarters into a total of 30 thin slices. Wrap the cantaloupe slices with prosciutto, covering the melon completely. Set the cantaloupe aside.

Slice the crusts from the bread and cut the bread slices into 3- x 3-inch (7.5 x 7.5 cm) squares. Spread the cream cheese mixture on the bread. Hold back enough cream cheese for a garnish.

Place 3 wrapped cantaloupe slices on each piece of the bread, side by side. Trim the overhanging cantaloupe. Cut the bread into 3 slices, or "fingers." Place a small mint leaf on the end of each finger. Place the remaining cream cheese mixture into a piping bag. Pipe a dollop of the cream cheese mixture on top of the end of the mint leaf, holding it down. The mint leaf should be showing. Do this for each bread finger. Lay the fingers on a flat serving platter. Serve them at room temperature. Or cover them and refrigerate them until they're needed, but no more than 2 hours. Let them warm to room temperature before you serve them.

building blocks
The predominant building block is sweetness from the cantaloupe and raisins. An off-dry white has enough sweetness to match.

flavors
Choose an off-dry white with tropical flavors to harmonize with the flavors of cantaloupe and raisins.

stuffed baguette with chicken, pineapple & walnut spread

Chicken and pineapple are a classic harmonizing combination, falling under the category of tantric twosomes.

Serves 4–6 (makes 12 rounds)

½ lb	250 g	cream cheese, at room temperature
1½ cups	375 mL	finely chopped cooked chicken
⅔ cup	150 mL	crushed pineapple, well drained
		sea salt to taste
		freshly ground black pepper to taste
¼ cup	50 mL	chopped toasted walnuts*
1		baguette
		pimento-stuffed olives (for garnish)

*To toast walnuts, toss them in a dry skillet over medium heat.

Mix the cream cheese, chicken and pineapple well in a bowl. Season the mixture with salt and pepper. Fold in the walnuts. Refrigerate the mixture for several hours or overnight.

Slice off the ends of the baguette. Cut the baguette in thirds so you have 3 (6 inch/15 cm) loaves. Using a long, sharp knife, hollow out the inside of 1 loaf, leaving a thin bread crust. Using the back of a spoon, push the dough out of the loaf. Stand 1 end of the loaf on a flat work surface. Using a spoon, pack the empty loaf with chicken spread. Repeat twice. Wrap the stuffed loaves in foil and refrigerate them for several hours to set.

Before serving, slice the loaves into ½-inch-thick (1 cm) rounds. Use an extra-sharp serrated knife for clean, straight edges. Slice the olives in half. Place a half olive in the center of each baguette round. Arrange the rounds on a platter. Cover and refrigerate them until they're needed.

building blocks
The predominant building blocks are fattiness from the cream cheese and sweetness from the pineapple. An off-dry white is ideal.

flavors
Choose an off-dry white with tropical notes to harmonize with the pineapple.

orgasmic appetizers to pair with dry & off-dry rosés

dry & off-dry rosés

PREDOMINANT BUILDING BLOCKS:

In dry versions, sourness and fruitiness, sometimes with hint of pleasant bitterness.

In off-dry versions, a balance of sourness, fruitiness and some sweetness.

FLAVORS:

In dry versions, sour fruit, such as sour cherries or cranberries, sometimes flavors of mineral and herbal notes.

In off-dry versions, ripe berry fruit flavors, such as strawberry and cherry. Flavors can sometimes be reminiscent of candy apples or candy floss.

WINES PRODUCED IN THE ROSÉ STYLE

- Rosés are the ideal wine style for daytime sipping and barbecue evenings.

- They range in color from salmon to pink to near purple, depending on how long the grapes stay in contact with the skins during the fermentation process. In general, the wine is fermented on its skins for a short time.

- Rosés can be light- to medium-bodied and can be dry, off-dry or sweet.

- Wines in this style can offer a hint of pleasant bitterness on the finish.

- Rosés are good partners for casual and comfort dining, cold pasta salads, cold cuts and barbe-cued foods.

The regions at right are stylistically noted for producing dry and off-dry rosés.

REGIONS

dry rosé
Canada (British Columbia, Ontario)

Chile

France (Languedoc, Provence, Southern Côtes du Rhône, Tavel, Southern Rhône)

Greece

Italy (Bardolino)

Spain (Catalonia, Navarra)

off-dry rosé
Canada (British Columbia, Ontario)

others
Mateus Rosé — Portugal

White Zinfandel — United States (California)

hot & spicy buffalo chicken dip

I love hot and spicy Buffalo wings accompanied by a blue cheese dip. They're classic pub food, often served with beer. Buffalo wings themselves are too intense to pair with a table wine. But since they're one of my favorite appetizers, I wanted to create a wine-savvy dip that celebrates traditional Buffalo wing flavor and heat in combination with blue cheese.

Serves 4–6

6		whole wheat pitas
8 oz	250 g	cream cheese
6 oz	175 g	cooked diced chicken breasts
½ cup	125 mL	mild hot sauce
8 oz	250 g	crumbled blue cheese
¼ cup	50 mL	chopped green onion (for garnish)

Preheat the oven to 375°F (190°C). With a serrated knife, separate the layers of each pita. Stack 2 or 3 layers together and cut them into quarters, or eighths, if you prefer. Spread the wedges out on 2 large rimmed baking sheets sprayed with nonstick cooking spray. Bake them for about 20 minutes, or until the pieces are golden. Cool them completely.

Preheat the oven to 350°F (180°C). Spread the cream cheese over the bottom of a small, ovenproof casserole dish. Combine the chicken cubes and hot sauce in a small bowl. Spread the chicken mixture evenly over the cream cheese. Top the chicken with crumbled blue cheese. Transfer the dip to the oven and bake it for 10 minutes, or until the blue cheese has melted and the dip is heated through. Sprinkle this dip with green onions. Serve it hot with pita wedges.

building blocks
The predominant building block is heat and spice from the wing sauce. An off-dry rosé with lots of sweetness offsets the heat and spice.

flavors
Choose an off-dry rosé with herbal notes to highlight the subtle flavor of the green onion.

baked goat cheese canapés with fennel

The delicate flavor and weight of goat cheese call for canapé ingredients with equal or less of the same. If the other ingredients are too heavy and flavorful, the rest of the canapé will dominate the goat cheese. In other words, pumpernickel and other heavy breads won't work here. Make sure to keep the goat cheese cold, otherwise it will crumble.

Serves 4–6
(makes 12 rounds)

1		log soft-ripened goat cheese (10 oz/300 g)
2		eggs
½ cup	125 mL	Italian dried breadcrumbs
1 Tbsp	15 mL	fennel seeds*
		sea salt to taste
		freshly ground black pepper to taste
1		package rice crackers

* Toast the fennel seeds in a dry skillet until they're aromatic. Remove them from the heat and let them cool.

Preheat the oven to 350°F (180°C). Keeping the hot water running, use it to heat a sharp knife. Cut the goat cheese log into 12 equal medallions, cleaning and warming the knife between slices. Beat the eggs in a bowl. Combine the breadcrumbs, fennel seeds and salt and pepper to taste in another. Dip the goat cheese rounds into the egg, then dredge them on all sides in breadcrumbs. Place the slices on a rimmed baking sheet sprayed with nonstick cooking spray. Bake the rounds for 5 to 7 minutes, until the breadcrumbs are golden and crisp. Place 1 round onto each rice cracker. Serve the appetizer warm.

building blocks
The predominant building block is sourness from the fresh goat cheese. A dry rosé has enough sourness to match the cheese.

flavors
Choose a dry rosé with herbal notes to draw out the subtle flavor of the fennel.

mini curried sweet potato latkes with mint, applesauce & sour cream

These tiny bites are so cute! They also please the palate and the pocketbook.

Serves 4–6 (makes 36 latkes)

2		medium-sized sweet potatoes, peeled
½		onion, finely diced
3		eggs
1 cup	250 mL	finely ground unsalted crackers (or matzo meal)
1 tsp	5 mL	curry powder
1 Tbsp	15 mL	brown sugar
½ tsp	2 mL	garam masala
¼ tsp	1 mL	cumin
		sea salt to taste
		freshly ground black pepper to taste
2 Tbsp	25 mL	finely chopped fresh mint
		corn oil (for frying)
		applesauce (for garnish)
		sour cream (for garnish)

building blocks
The predominant building block is sweetness from the sweet potatoes, brown sugar and applesauce. An off-dry rosé has enough sweetness to match. The wine's sweetness also nicely offsets the spiciness of the curry.

flavors
Choose an off-dry rosé with strawberry tones to complement the apple flavor.

Grate the sweet potatoes by hand or in a food processor with a shredder blade. Combine them with the onion, eggs, ground crackers, curry powder, brown sugar, garam masala and cumin. Season the mixture with salt and pepper. Fold in the mint.

Pour some oil into a large skillet, about ¼ inch (5 mm) up the sides. Heat the oil until it's hot but not smoking. Lightly pack together about ¼ cup (50 mL) of the onion mixture. Drop it onto the skillet and flatten it slightly. Repeat the process until the skillet is almost full, leaving about 1 inch (2.5 cm) between the latkes. Fry them, flipping them halfway through, until their edges are golden and crisp, about 1 minute per side. Pat each latke down with the back of your spatula and drain it on paper towel. Repeat this process until all the mixture is used up. Set the latkes on a plate and garnish each with a dollop of applesauce and a dollop of sour cream. Serve them warm or at room temperature.

sweet jerk grilled pineapple dip

A good friend of mine, Chef David Franklin, developed this recipe using my Orgasmic Culinary Creations Sweet Jerk dry rub. I make this dip and take it to some of the local gourmet food stores that sell my dry rub. Store customers try the dip, moan and then purchase a package of the dry rub. It's a crowd-pleaser.

Serves 4–6

4		½-inch-thick (1 cm) pineapple slices, peeled and cored
1		large shallot, peeled and cut in half, root intact
2 Tbsp	25 mL	honey, heated
1 Tbsp	15 mL	canola or other neutral-flavored oil
½ cup	125 mL	Orgasmic Culinary Creations Sweet Jerk dry rub*
1 lb	500 g	cream cheese, at room temperature
2 Tbsp	25 mL	green onion, minced
1 Tbsp	15 mL	cilantro, finely chopped
		plantain chips, tortilla chips, crostini or flatbreads for dipping

*Turn to the last page for more details on how to purchase Sweet Jerk, or substitute with homemade Jamaican Seasoning (see page 219).

Preheat a gas or charcoal grill. Toss the pineapple and shallot with the honey and oil in a large bowl. Sprinkle in the Sweet Jerk to evenly coat the mixture. Grill the pineapple and shallot until they're nicely browned. Place them in a clean bowl to cool.

When they're cool, dice the pineapple and shallot and fold them into the softened cream cheese. Stir in the green onion and cilantro. Add more Sweet Jerk, if necessary, to your personal taste. Place the dip in a serving bowl and chill it in the refrigerator for at least 2 hours to allow the flavors to meld. Serve it with plantain chips, tortilla chips, crostini or flatbreads.

building blocks
The predominant building blocks are sweetness from the pineapple and heat and spice from the Sweet Jerk. The sweetness of an off-dry rosé harmonizes with the pineapple and nicely offsets the heat and spice.

flavors
Choose an off-dry rosé with tropical flavors to work with the pineapple flavor.

crispy pork balls with pineapple dipping sauce

I made these little treats for my mom and dad. My dad and I are nontasters; my mom's a super-taster. Yet we all decided this recipe most definitely falls into the category of mouth-watering.

Serves 4–6 (makes 24 balls)

Pineapple dipping sauce:

½ cup	125 mL	pineapple jam
2 Tbsp	25 mL	freshly squeezed lime juice
½ tsp	2 mL	chili paste

Pork balls:

1 cup	250 mL	dried egg noodles
1 lb	500 g	minced pork
1		small onion, minced
3		cloves garlic, minced
1 inch	2.5 cm	piece fresh ginger, peeled and grated
½ cup	125 mL	finely chopped fresh cilantro
1		egg
½ cup	125 mL	all-purpose flour
½ tsp	2 mL	chili paste
1 tsp	5 mL	fish sauce
		corn oil (for deep-frying)
		toothpicks

building blocks
The predominant building blocks are heat and spice from the chili paste and sweetness from the pineapple in the dipping sauce. An off-dry rosé with sweetness offsets the heat and spice while it harmonizes with the dipping sauce.

flavors
Choose a rosé with tropical notes to match the flavor of pineapple.

Combine the pineapple jam, lime juice and chili paste in a small bowl. Cover it and refrigerate it until it's needed.

Put the dried egg noodles in a bowl and cover them with boiling water. Let them stand for 5 to 7 minutes or until they're soft. Drain them and set them aside.

Mix the remaining pork ball ingredients together in a large bowl. Add the drained noodles. Mix them together well. Roll about 1 tsp (5 mL) of the pork mixture into a bite-sized meatball. Repeat until all the pork mixture is used up.

In a large pot or skillet over high heat, heat the oil to 375°F (190°C). Deep-fry the pork balls in batches, 7 to 10 minutes, turning them frequently until all their sides are golden. Drain them on paper towels. Arrange them on a platter and serve the pork balls hot or at room temperature with toothpicks and the dipping sauce.

lip-smacking, finger-lickin', good & messy ribs

Since you're serving these ribs as an appetizer, be sure to make them the night before. Let the ribs cool to room temperature. Cover them with foil and refrigerate them overnight. You may need extra napkins for this one!

Serves 4–6

5½ lb	2.5 kg	baby back pork ribs*
1		bottle ale

Dry rub:

1 Tbsp	15 mL	coarse sea salt
2 Tbsp	25 mL	brown sugar
1 Tbsp	15 mL	freshly ground black pepper
1 tsp	5 mL	dried mustard
2 Tbsp	25 mL	paprika
2 Tbsp	25 mL	olive oil

Sauce:

1 cup	250 mL	ketchup
2 Tbsp	25 mL	Dijon mustard
2 Tbsp	25 mL	balsamic vinegar
2 Tbsp	25 mL	Japanese soy sauce
2 Tbsp	25 mL	molasses
1		bulb garlic, roasted

*Have your butcher remove the membrane on the ribs.

Preheat the oven to 350°F (180°C). Wash the ribs under cold water. Pat them dry. Pour the ale into the bottom of a roasting pan. Cut the ribs to fit onto the broiler rack of the roasting pan. Combine all the rub ingredients, except for the oil, in a bowl. Coat the ribs with the oil, then sprinkle them with the rub. Set them aside.

Combine all the sauce ingredients in a small skillet and simmer the sauce on low heat for 15 minutes, stirring occasionally. Set aside.

Cover the ribs with foil, set on the pan and roast for 1 hour. Reduce the heat to 275°F (120°C) and roast them for another 30 minutes. Remove the foil. Coat the ribs with the sauce and bake for another 30 minutes, until the sauce is caramelized. Remove the ribs from the oven. Let them cool. (Do not cut the ribs.) Refrigerate, covered, overnight.

The next day, cut the ribs before reheating them to keep the meat from falling off the bone. Set the cut ribs on a rimmed baking sheet sprayed with nonstick cooking spray. Cover them with more sauce and heat them for about 15 minutes in a 350°F (180°C) preheated oven. Serve them on a platter with more sauce.

building blocks
The predominant building block is sweetness, due to the brown sugar and molasses. An off-dry rosé has enough sweetness to match.

flavors
Choose an off-dry rosé with lots of dark berry fruit flavors to match the depth of earthy flavor in molasses.

mini whole wheat thai pizzettas

The pizza crusts, sauce and toppings can be made in advance, even the night before. This is a delicious Thai version of an Italian classic. It's a heavy appetizer, so two slices per person are enough.

Serves 4–6 (makes 12 pizzettas)

Pizza dough:

2¼ cups	550 mL	whole wheat flour
½ tsp	2 mL	sugar
½ tsp	2 mL	sea salt
2 tsp	10 mL	quick-rising yeast
1 Tbsp	15 mL	olive oil
¾ cup	175 mL	warm water
		cornmeal (as needed)

Base sauce:

1 cup	250 mL	chunky peanut butter
1 cup	250 mL	unsweetened coconut milk
2 Tbsp	25 mL	light soy sauce
½ tsp	2 mL	chili paste

Toppings:

12		cooked shrimp, peeled and finely chopped
2		green onions, diced
⅓ cup	75 mL	fresh basil, finely chopped
¼		red pepper, diced
2 cups	500 mL	shredded mozzarella cheese
12		cooked whole shrimp, tails removed (for garnish)

building blocks

The predominant building blocks are sweetness from the peanut butter and coconut milk and heat and spice from the sauce. An off-dry rosé has enough sweetness to harmonize with the sweetness of the sauce and offset the heat and spice.

flavors

Choose an off-dry rosé with tropical flavors to draw out the coconut flavor of the peanut sauce.

Preheat the oven to 350°F (180°C). To make the pizza dough, combine 2 cups (500 mL) of the flour, the sugar, salt, yeast and olive oil in a large bowl. Make a well in the center of the flour and add the warm water. Using a fork, mix this together; it will begin to form a soft dough. Turn the dough onto a clean work surface and knead it until it's elastic-like, about 10 minutes. Use extra flour if needed. Set the dough in a bowl, cover it with a damp cloth and let it stand in a warm place for 45 minutes.

Cut the dough into 12 pieces. Roll out 1 piece into a 3-inch-diameter (7.5 cm) circle. Use a 2-inch (5 cm) cookie cutter or the rim of a wine class to cut the dough out into mini pizzas, uniform in size and shape. Spray a pizza pan with nonstick cooking spray. Sprinkle it with cornmeal. Set the mini pizzas on the pan. Parbake them in the oven for 5 to 7 minutes or until the bottoms of the pizzas are parcooked (but not golden). Remove them from the oven. Let them cool.

To make the sauce, combine the peanut butter, coconut milk, soy sauce and chili paste in a skillet. Cook the mixture over low heat, stirring it until it thickens. Remove it from the heat and let it cool.

Combine the chopped shrimp, green onions, basil and red pepper in a bowl. Place 1 Tbsp (15 mL) of sauce on each pizza crust (you won't want it any thicker). Top the sauce with the shrimp mixture. Sprinkle each pizza with a generous amount of mozzarella. Place 1 whole shrimp on top of the mozzarella.

Place the pizzas on the pizza pan, 6 at a time. Bake them for 10 to 15 minutes, or until the crust is golden and the mozzarella is melted. Serve the pizzas hot.

multigrain pizza crusts

Multigrain pizza crust adds an additional layer of interesting, earthy flavor and chewy and crunchy texture. When buying multigrain flour, make sure the ingredient list on the bag contains whole grains, preferably stone-ground. This flour tends to be lumpy, giving the pizza dough less elasticity than a traditional one.

Instead of stretching the dough to fit the pan, I work with it like it's a pie crust. I place the dough on a well-floured work surface and roll it out with a rolling pin. This method makes the crust even and thin. Too thick a crust is heavy and too hard to chew. Placing the pizza pan over the dough, I cut the dough around it. This creates a perfect, symmetrical fit. I sprinkle the pizza pan with cornmeal before placing the dough on top. I parbake the crust in a preheated 475°F (240°C) oven for about four minutes. Parbaking ensures your crust will be firm enough to hold wet or heavy ingredients.

After spreading the crust with tomato sauce, I sprinkle the top with wild mushrooms, chopped onion, fresh rosemary, cubes of brie and shredded mozzarella. I bake the pizza at 400°F (200°C) for about 15 minutes, until the multigrain crust is golden.

Usually I consider pizza to be a casual dish, ideally served with easy-drinking, inexpensive wines. But in the case of a multigrain crust, if it's topped with fresh, high-quality ingredients, you can cut your pizza into wedges and serve it as an appetizer or entrée with a well-made white or red wine.

How about multigrain pizzettas topped with basic tomato sauce, artichoke hearts, basil pesto, fresh oregano and fresh buffalo mozzarella? The ideal wine partner to work with the fattiness of pesto on this pizza is a big, fat white with lots of creamy texture. Its background hints of toast and oak harmonize well with the background earthy notes of a multigrain crust.

A multigrain pizzetta topped with pancetta, kalamata olives and cheddar cheese needs a full-flavored red wine as a partner. Only a big red will stand up to the saltiness of pancetta, the bitterness of olives and the sharp flavor of cheddar cheese.

sticky mandarin mini fried drumlets

Appetizers that force us to eat with our hands help create an intimate and sensual environment. This fun appetizer is worthy of public finger-licking. I tested the recipe on students in my wine certificate program at Fleming College and they gave the recipe two sticky thumbs up!

Serves 4–6
(makes 30 drumlets)

Sticky mandarin coating:

1 cup	250 mL	brown sugar
1 cup	250 mL	rice vinegar
½ cup	125 mL	water
½ cup	125 mL	pineapple juice
¼ cup	50 mL	ketchup
1 Tbsp	15 mL	Chinese light soy sauce
1 Tbsp	15 mL	cornstarch (dissolved in water)
		sea salt to taste
		freshly ground black pepper to taste

Seasoned flour:

1 cup	250 mL	all-purpose flour
1 tsp	5 mL	garlic powder
		sea salt to taste
		freshly ground black pepper to taste
2		eggs, beaten
30		chicken wings, winglet and tips removed*
		corn oil (for deep-frying)
		sesame seeds (for garnish)

*If possible, use 2 lb (1 kg) of chicken wings. Order the wings in advance from your local butcher. Have the butcher remove the winglets and tips. This will save you a lot of time. Keep the winglets for another use.

To make the sticky coating, combine all the ingredients in a skillet over low heat, then bring it to a boil over high heat. Reduce the heat to low again and let the sauce simmer for 15 minutes, until it's thickened. Remove it from the heat and set it aside.

To make the seasoned flour, mix the flour, garlic powder, salt and pepper together in a medium bowl. Set it aside. Beat the eggs in a third bowl. Set it aside.

To make the drumlets, in a circular motion, run a sharp paring knife around the top of the thick bone to loosen the flesh. Push the flesh down on all sides around the bone toward the fleshy end. Once the flesh is pushed down, it should resemble a mini drumstick. Clean the bone of any flesh. Dip the mini drumlets into the egg, then dredge

continued on next page

them in the seasoned flour. Coat them completely. Set the drumlets on a platter, cover them and refrigerate them for 2 to 3 hours. By letting them air-dry, you reduce the spattering of the oil and help make them crispier. (You may need to coat them a second time in the seasoned flour after removing them from the refrigerator.)

Preheat the oven to 350°F (180°C). Heat the oil to 375°F (190°C) in a deep-fryer or a deep pot. Deep-fry several drumlets at a time. The drumlets are done when the frying noise has abated somewhat and they're floating. Drain them on paper towel.

Place the drumlets in a shallow baking dish. Pour the sticky mixture over them, coating them completely. Bake the drumlets until they're hot, about 30 minutes. Sprinkle them with sesame seeds. Pile them onto a platter and serve them hot or at room temperature. Make sure to supply plenty of napkins.

building blocks
The predominant building block is sweetness due to the pine-apple and brown sugar. An off-dry rosé is perfect.

flavors
Choose an off-dry rosé with candy apple flavors to complement the candied coating.

smoked bacon–wrapped dates stuffed with rosemary sausage

I made this appetizer for my husband and me to sample. Jack rarely eats bacon; he said he only wanted one or two of these tasty bites to test. Before the end of the evening, he had consumed the entire plate, claiming he couldn't stop as they were highly addictive. I knew then that this finger food was destined for this book.

Serves 4–6 (makes 32 wrapped dates)

16		slices smoked bacon, halved
2		pork sausages (6 inches/15 cm long)
4 oz	125 g	cream cheese
½ tsp	2 mL	dried rosemary
		sea salt and freshly ground black pepper to taste
32		fresh dates, pitted*
		toothpicks

*When you pit the dates yourself, they have a nice clean cavity.

Preheat the oven to 350°F (180°C). Arrange the bacon in a single layer on a rimmed baking sheet sprayed with nonstick cooking spray and partially cook it in the oven for about 5 minutes, so it's still pliable. Remove it, drain it on paper towel and cut each slice in half. Remove the sausages from their casings and cook the meat in a skillet over medium heat. Remove the sausage from the skillet and drain off the fat.

Combine the cooked sausage, cream cheese, rosemary and salt and pepper in a bowl, mixing it together well. Cut the dates open, butterfly style. Stuff each date with ½ tsp (2 mL) of the sausage mixture. Roll each date in a half slice of bacon. Place the rolled dates on a rimmed baking sheet sprayed with nonstick cooking spray. Bake the dates at 350°F (180°C) until the bacon is crispy, about 20 minutes. Drain them on paper towel. Arrange them on a serving platter and put a toothpick into each one.

building blocks
The predominant building block is fattiness from the bacon and cream cheese and sweetness from the dates. Choose an off-dry rosé with some sweetness to harmonize with the dates.

flavors
Choose an off-dry rosé with herbal flavors to contrast with the fruitiness of the dates.

prosciutto-wrapped figs with gorgonzola & walnuts

A wonderful combination of contrasting textures and flavors—between the crispy prosciutto and the soft, sweet figs—is found in these tiny gems.

*Serves 4–6
(makes 12 figs)*

3 Tbsp	40 mL	Gorgonzola cheese
4 oz	125 g	cream cheese
12		large fresh figs, stems removed*
12		toasted walnut pieces**
12		thin strips of shaved prosciutto

*If fresh figs are out of season, use dried ones. Place the dried figs in a bowl of water, cover it and refrigerate the figs for 24 hours.

**Walnuts can be toasted in a dry skillet over medium heat, tossing them frequently, for about 3 minutes.

Preheat the broiler. Combine the Gorgonzola and cream cheese in a bowl. Butterfly each fig. Place a walnut piece inside the fig. Put a dollop of cheese mixture on top of the walnut. Roll the fig up in prosciutto.

Spray a rimmed baking sheet with nonstick cooking spray. Place the figs on it, seam side down. Broil the figs until the prosciutto is crispy, about 2 minutes. Turn the figs over and broil them for about 1 minute longer, to crisp the other side. Watch the figs carefully to avoid burning them. Remove the figs from the oven. Arrange them on a platter and serve them hot with napkins.

building blocks
The predominant building blocks are sweetness from the figs and saltiness from the prosciutto and Gorgonzola. The sweetness in an off-dry rosé harmonizes with the natural sweetness in figs. The wine's sourness nicely offsets the saltiness.

flavors
Choose an off-dry rosé with dried fruit flavors to complement the figs.

shrimp wrapped in wontons with plum sauce

The crunchy wonton wrapper contrasts with the soft texture of the shrimp, adding an extra layer of mouthfeel.

Serves 4–6 (makes 24 shrimp)

24		raw shrimp, peeled, deveined, tails on
1 tsp	5 mL	cornstarch
1 tsp	5 mL	water
24		wonton wrappers
		corn oil (for frying)
½ cup	125 mL	plum sauce (facing page)

Wash the shrimp. Pat them dry. Mix together the cornstarch and water in a small bowl. Fold each wonton wrapper in half to form a triangle. Keep the triangles covered with a damp cloth while you're working with them. Wrap a triangle around each shrimp. Brush the cornstarch mixture on the end of each wrapper to seal it. Put the wrapped shrimp on a plate, cover it and refrigerate the shrimp for half an hour.

Pour enough oil to cover the shrimp in a large skillet over high heat. When the oil is hot, fry 1 wonton shrimp until the wrapper is golden, about 5 seconds. Test it to make sure the shrimp is cooked. Cook the shrimp in batches. Drain them on paper towel. Serve the wontons hot or at room temperature with the dipping sauce.

building blocks
The predominant building blocks are sweetness from the plum jam and heat and spice from the chili. An off-dry rosé has enough sweetness to match and to offset the gentle heat and spice.

flavors
Choose an off-dry rosé with pitted fruit flavors to match the flavor of the plum sauce.

Plum sauce:

1 cup	250 mL	plum jam
1 Tbsp	15 mL	rice vinegar
1 tsp	5 mL	onion powder
½ tsp	2 mL	finely chopped fresh ginger
¼ tsp	1 mL	allspice
¼ tsp	1 mL	chili with fried garlic*
¼ cup	50 mL	water
		mint sprigs (for garnish)

*Chili with fried garlic is available at Asian supermarkets.

Combine all the ingredients in a small pot over high heat. Bring the mixture to a boil. Reduce the heat and simmer the sauce for 5 minutes. Add more water if it gets too thick. Transfer the sauce to a bowl. Cover it and refrigerate it until it's needed. Garnish with sprigs of fresh mint.

*orgasmic
appetizers
to pair
with light,
fruity reds*

Light, fruity reds

PREDOMINANT BUILDING BLOCKS:
Sourness and fruitiness, sometimes with pleasant bitterness.

FLAVORS:
Cherry, strawberry and gooseberry; sometimes spicy and mineral-like flavors.

WINES PRODUCED IN THE LIGHT, FRUITY RED STYLE

- One of the most famous wines in the world falls into this style—red Burgundy

- Light, fruity reds may be light- to medium-bodied, but aren't simple. They can offer fantastic depth and layers of flavors (complexity), good structure and a long, lasting finish.

- In North America, the most prestigious wines produced in this style are Pinot Noirs, mostly in cooler climatic regions. This climate gives the resulting wines elegance, finesse and sophistication as well as great acidity.

- Gamay Noir is another grape variety that produces easy-drinking versions in this light, fruity style.

- Best food matches include fatty fish, such as salmon and swordfish, chicken, quail, squab, feta, goat cheese, beets, cabbage, whole wheat pasta and wild mushrooms.

The regions at right are stylistically noted for producing light, fruity reds.

REGIONS

gamay
Canada (British Columbia, Ontario)
France (Beaujolais, Languedoc)

pinot noir
Canada (British Columbia, Ontario)
France (Burgundy)
United States (California, Oregon, Washington State)

mini whole wheat focaccia with sun-dried cherries & toasted walnuts & rosemary

There's nothing more rustic and scrumptious than a hunk of freshly baked bread and a glass of red wine. What's handy about this treat is that all the ingredients, with the exception of the olive oil, can be purchased in a small quantity at a bulk food store and are therefore quite inexpensive.

Serves 4–6 (makes 12 focaccia)

½ lb	250 g	sun-dried cherries*
1 tsp	5 mL	white sugar
¾ cup	175 mL	warm water (more if needed)
1		package active dry yeast
3 cups	750 mL	whole wheat flour
1 tsp	5 mL	sea salt
1 tsp	5 mL	freshly ground black pepper
2 Tbsp	25 mL	finely chopped fresh rosemary
3 Tbsp	40 mL	olive oil
¼ cup	50 mL	toasted walnut pieces**
		olive oil (as needed)

*Sun-dried cherries are available at most bulk food stores.

**Walnuts can be toasted in a dry skillet over medium heat, tossing them frequently, for about 3 minutes.

Place the cherries in a bowl with just enough water to cover them. Let them sit until they're needed. Dissolve the sugar in the warm water in another bowl. Sprinkle it with yeast. Let the yeast and sugar stand for 10 minutes, until they're foaming.

Combine the yeast mixture with the flour in a large bowl. Add the salt, pepper and rosemary. Stir in more water if needed, 1 Tbsp (15 mL) at a time. Using a fork, mix the dough together. The dough should be gooey, not dry. When it has pulled together, oil your hands with olive oil, pick up the dough and throw it back into the bowl. Do this about 20 times. This process helps to bind the dough. If the dough is stuck to your hands, this means it's gooey enough. Lightly oil a large bowl. Place the dough in the bowl and coat it with oil. Cover it with a damp cloth and let it stand in a warm place until it has doubled in volume, about 1 hour.

Preheat the oven to 475°F (240°C). Drain the cherries. Punch the dough and turn it out onto a lightly floured clean work surface. Divide the dough into 12 equally sized balls. Roll out each ball into a mini focaccia, about 3 inches (7.5 cm) in diameter. Brush the top with oil. Sprinkle each focaccia with the cherries and the walnut pieces. Press them into the dough. Coat a seasoned, cast iron skillet (12 inches/30 cm) in diameter with olive oil. Place 3 focacce (the plural of foccacia) in the cast iron skillet. Drizzle with more olive oil.

Bake the focacce for 10 to 20 minutes, or until the sides and top are golden. Transfer the focacce to a wire rack. Oil the skillet again and bake the focacce in batches, 3 at a time. Serve them warm or at room temperature.

building blocks
The predominant building blocks are sourness from the cherries and bitterness from the walnut pieces. A light, fruity red has enough sourness and bitterness to match.

flavors
Choose a light, fruity red with sour cherry flavor to harmonize with the flavor of the sun-dried cherries.

chicken-stuffed mushroom caps

This is a simple appetizer featuring classic flavors. It's always a good idea to have a few appetizers of this style at every event for your conservative dining pals.

Serves 4–6 (makes 16 caps)

16		large button mushrooms
¾ cup	175 mL	butter
¼ cup	50 mL	diced onion
1½ lb	750 g	chicken, cooked and finely chopped
2 Tbsp	25 mL	dry sherry
2 Tbsp	25 mL	chicken stock
1 cup	250 mL	dried breadcrumbs
¼ cup	50 mL	finely chopped fresh basil
4 oz	125 g	freshly grated Gruyère

Preheat the oven to 350°F (180°C). Wipe the mushrooms and remove their stalks. Finely chop the stalks. Set them aside. Melt the butter in a large skillet and flip the mushrooms around in the melted butter but do not fry them. Remove the mushrooms and place them in a single layer on a rimmed baking dish sprayed with nonstick cooking spray.

Add the onion and the mushroom stalks to the remaining butter in the skillet. Sauté them until they're soft, about 2 minutes. Stir in the chicken and the sherry and add enough stock to bind the mixture together. Add the breadcrumbs. Fold in the basil. Remove the mixture from the heat. Drain off any excess liquid.

Place 1 tsp (5 mL) of the mixture in each mushroom cap. Sprinkle the mushrooms with Gruyère. Bake them for 7 to 10 minutes, until they're heated through and the cheese has melted. Gently remove them and arrange them on a platter. Serve them hot.

building blocks
The predominant building block is medium fattiness from the butter and Gruyère. A light, fruity red has just enough weight to match.

flavors
Choose a light, fruity red with earthy flavors to harmonize with the earthy nature of the mushrooms.

caramelized onion & goat cheese crostini

Chef Jeff Crump of the Ancaster Old Mill Restaurant in Ancaster, Ontario, prepared this stunning appetizer for my friend and me. The simple approach of separating the caramelized onion sweetness from the goat cheese tanginess—rather than layering them on top of each other—provides a truly orgasmic experience for the palate.

*Serves 4–6
(makes 24 crostini)*

¼ cup	50 mL	vegetable oil
1		clove garlic, minced
2		large onions, minced
2 Tbsp	25 mL	finely chopped fresh thyme
		sea salt to taste
		freshly ground black pepper to taste
1		baguette, frozen
2 cups	500 mL	extra virgin olive oil
8 oz	250 g	crumbled goat cheese
12		cherry tomatoes, halved
		extra virgin olive oil (for drizzling)

Heat the oil over low heat in a medium skillet and add the garlic and onions. Cook and stir this mixture until it's a deep, rich golden brown, about 30 minutes. This caramelization process is important to the appetizer's flavor. Add the thyme and season the onions with salt and pepper to taste. This mixture can be made up to 3 days in advance, covered and refrigerated.

Slice the frozen baguette, as thinly as possible, into 24 slices, using a sharp, serrated knife. Heat the olive oil in a large skillet until it's very hot but not smoking. Fry the bread slices until they're golden brown and transfer them to a plate lined with paper towel. Season the bread with salt.

To assemble, spread the cool onion mixture on half the fried bread. Sprinkle the other half with goat cheese. Top each side of the crostini with a cherry tomato half. Season the rounds with salt and pepper. Drizzle them with olive oil. Serve them warm or at room temperature.

building blocks
The predominant building blocks in this recipe are sourness from the goat cheese and sweetness from the caramelized onion. A light, fruity red with a backbone of sourness matches the sourness of goat cheese. Ripe fruitiness harmonizes with the sweetness of the caramelized onion.

flavors
Choose a light, fruity red with sour cherry flavor to match the flavor of the goat cheese.

smoky ham & provolone sliders

While visiting Culver, Indiana, I tried a "slider" for the first time. A slider is a mini sandwich that slides easily into your mouth in one or two bites and just as easily into your tummy. Here's my slider recipe, influenced by my love of the ham and cheese sandwich.

Serves 4–6 (makes 8 sliders)

| 16 | | slices of smoked ham |
| 8 | | thin slices of smoked provolone cheese |

Batter:

1		egg
1 tsp	5 mL	vegetable oil
		sea salt to taste
		freshly ground black pepper to taste
1 cup	250 mL	dried breadcrumbs
⅓ cup	75 mL	all-purpose flour
¼ cup	50 mL	corn oil
2 Tbsp	25 mL	butter

Preheat the oven to 400°F (200°C). Cut the ham and provolone into slices that are 2 x 2 inches (5 x 5 cm) in diameter and ⅛ inch (3 mm) thick. Lay out 8 pieces of the ham and cover each with a slice of provolone. Top with the other piece of ham and press these breadless "sandwiches" together.

Combine the egg, oil, salt and pepper in a bowl. Set the mixture aside. Combine the breadcrumbs and flour in another bowl. Dredge each ham and cheese square in egg and then roll it in the breadcrumb mixture. Pat the breadcrumbs neatly into the ham squares. Set them on a rimmed baking sheet sprayed with nonstick cooking spray. Cover and refrigerate them for 30 minutes. Heat the oil and the butter in a large skillet over medium heat. Fry the sliders for 2 to 3 minutes per side, or until they're golden brown. Serve them hot.

building blocks
The predominant building blocks are saltiness from the ham and fattiness from the cheese. A light, fruity red has enough sourness to offset the saltiness and enough weight to stand up to the fat in cheese.

flavors
Choose a light, fruity red with smoky notes to draw out the subtle flavor of the smoked ham and smoked provolone.

roasted greek cheese canapés

Greek feta is made from sheep and goat's milk and offers us a tangy, salty alternative to blander cheeses. Cow's milk feta is almost as flavorful, but not quite as tangy or salty. You can use cow's milk feta for this appetizer, but if you do, choose a well-balanced, medium-bodied white wine to go with it.

Serves 4–6 (makes 12 canapés)

12		slices whole wheat bread
		corn oil (for frying)
2		large pieces of firm Greek feta cheese
¼ cup	50 mL	finely chopped fresh oregano
		fresh ground black pepper to taste
		olive oil (as needed)

Cut 12 circles out of the bread, using a 3-inch (7.5 cm) cookie cutter. Heat the olive oil in a skillet over medium heat. Fry the bread until it's golden on both sides, about 30 seconds per side. Drain it on paper towel.

Preheat the oven to 375°F (190°C). Spray a 12-cup muffin tin with nonstick cooking spray. Remove the feta from its whey and set it on a paper towel to drain. Cut the feta into 12 equal slices, each about ½ inch (1 cm) thick. Place a slice of feta in each cavity of the muffin tin. Sprinkle oregano over the cheese. Season it with black pepper. Drizzle it with olive oil. Cook the feta for 12 to 15 minutes, or until the cheese is melted. Remove the tin from the oven. Let the cheese cool slightly. Spoon out the feta from the tins and place it on the toasts. Serve them warm.

building blocks
The predominant building block is sourness from the feta. A light, fruity red has enough sourness to match.

flavors
Choose a light, fruity red with sour cherry flavors to complement the flavors of feta.

prosciutto-wrapped grilled ravioli

This is an appetizer I've enjoyed many times while dining at Riverside Grill, located in the Holiday Inn in Peterborough, Ontario. I decided to ask my friend, the hotel accountant, Grant Zwarych, if I could obtain the recipe for my cookbook. I was delighted to learn that Grant had actually developed the recipe and he willingly shared it with me. This is supereasy to produce and the ravioli is wonderful. This appetizer is best served hot, right off the grill. Reheating will make the ravioli hard and unpalatable.

Serves 4–6 (makes 6 ravioli)

24	fresh spinach and ricotta ravioli (2 x 2 inches/5 x 5 cm)
	olive oil (as needed)
	sea salt to taste
	freshly ground black pepper to taste
24	prosciutto slices (¼ inch/5 mm), halved
6	bamboo skewers (6 inch/15 cm), soaked overnight in water (soak some extras just in case; they're cheap)

Blanch the ravioli for about 1 minute in a large pot of boiling, salted water. Drain the pasta. Pour some olive oil into a bowl, season it with salt and pepper and gently toss the ravioli in it. Wrap 1 ravioli in 1 slice of prosciutto. (Use a skewer to secure the prosciutto.) Thread 4 of the wrapped ravioli on a skewer. Repeat for all 6 skewers.

Prepare the barbecue for medium-heat grilling. Grill the ravioli skewers for about 2 minutes per side, until the prosciutto is crisp and the ravioli is lightly golden on both sides. Serve hot.

building blocks
The predominant building block is saltiness from the prosciutto. A light, fruity red has enough sourness to offset the saltiness.

flavors
Choose a light, fruity red with mineral notes to highlight the delicate taste of spinach in the ravioli.

brie & walnut quesadillas with cranberry onion relish

If you're not a fan of the sour taste of cranberries and you sweeten the relish, be sure to partner the recipe with an off-dry rosé. This is a delightful recipe developed by my friend, Lisa Alguire.

Serves 4–6
(makes 12 slices)

Cranberry onion relish:

2 Tbsp	25 mL	corn oil
1		small onion, thinly sliced
2 tsp	10 mL	finely chopped fresh thyme
		sea salt to taste
		freshly ground black pepper to taste
½ cup	125 mL	dried cranberries
2 Tbsp	25 mL	dry white wine
1 Tbsp	15 mL	balsamic vinegar

Quesadillas:

4		multigrain tortillas (9 inches/23 cm in diameter)
8 oz	250 g	brie, thinly sliced
¾ cup	175 mL	chopped walnuts, toasted*
		corn oil (for frying)

*Walnuts can be toasted in a dry skillet over medium heat, tossing them frequently, for about 3 minutes.

To make the relish, heat 2 Tbsp (25 mL) oil in a skillet over medium heat. Sauté the onion, thyme, salt and pepper for about 20 minutes, until the onion is almost caramelized. Add the cranberries, wine and vinegar. Simmer the mixture until no liquid remains. Remove it from the heat. Transfer it to a dish and let it cool.

To make the quesadillas, cover 2 tortillas with slices of brie and sprinkle it with walnuts. Cover with another tortilla. Add 2 Tbsp (25 mL) of oil to the bottom of a large skillet. Heat the oil over medium heat. Fry the quesadillas until they're golden, about 1 to 2 minutes per side. Keep them warm. When you're ready to serve them, cut each into 6 slices. Serve them warm with a dipping bowl of Cranberry Onion Relish or place a dollop of the relish on each slice.

building blocks
The predominant building blocks are fattiness from the brie, bitterness from the walnuts and sourness from the relish. A light, fruity red has enough weight, bitterness and sourness to match.

flavors
Choose a light, fruity red with cherry tones to harmonize with the cranberry flavor.

sun-dried tomato tapenade

Tomatoes are high in basic umami. When sun-dried, they gain synthesized umami and double in flavor. This is an umami-rich, yet simple, appetizer.

Serves 4–6

6		whole wheat pitas
1 cup	250 mL	sun-dried tomatoes
2 cups	500 mL	boiling water
1 cup	250 mL	olive oil
3		cloves garlic, minced
½ cup	125 mL	capers

Preheat the oven to 375°F (190°C). With a serrated knife, separate the layers of each pita. Stack 2 or 3 layers together and cut the pitas into quarters, or eighths, if you prefer. Spread the wedges out on 2 large rimmed baking sheets sprayed with nonstick cooking spray. Bake them for about 20 minutes, or until the pieces are golden. Cool them completely.

Place the sun-dried tomatoes in a bowl and pour boiling water over them until they're just covered. Let them sit for 30 minutes, until the tomatoes are soft. Drain them. Place the sun-dried tomatoes and the remaining ingredients in a food processor or blender and purée them until they're blended. Transfer the tapenade to a bowl. Cover it and refrigerate it until it's needed, up to 8 hours. Serve with the toasted pita wedges.

building blocks
The predominant building blocks are fruitiness from the sun-dried tomatoes and saltiness from the capers. A light, fruity red has enough fruitiness to match the sun-dried tomatoes' fruitiness. The wine's sourness also offsets the saltiness of capers.

flavors
Choose a light, fruity red with cherry flavor to match the fruity flavor of the sun-dried tomatoes.

wine is healthy

Studies now show that red wine, consumed in moderation and with meals, contributes to a healthy lifestyle. So there's every reason to include red wine in your daily diet. You can cut down on fat, calories or carbohydrates and still enjoy a glass of the fermented red grape.

Research shows that when a person's diet is high in fat, drinking red wine with meals can mean a lower incidence of heart attacks. Many experts believe that red wine contains compounds, such as antioxidants, that aid in protecting our hearts and reducing the risk of strokes. Resveratrol is the most famous antioxidant in red wine, believed to be good at mopping up the chemicals responsible for causing blood clots, the primary cause of heart disease. Guercetin is another antioxidant that's thought to help prevent lung cancer. Red wine also has a flavonoid known as catechin that contributes to the reduction of heart attacks. Red wine is a natural tranquilizer, reduces anxiety and tension and aids in our digestion of food, adding minerals and vitamins to our bodies.

A glass of red wine is also okay if you're on a low-carbohydrate diet. A 3.5-ounce glass of red wine contains only 1.8 grams of net carbohydrates. If you're reducing your caloric intake, you'll be happy to know that this same glass of wine only contains 74 calories.

While always pleasant to include a glass of red wine with your evening meal, it's a sensual experience to choose one that harmonizes with your appetizers and entrée.

*orgasmic
appetizers
to pair with
reds with
forward fruit*

Reds with forward fruit

PREDOMINANT BUILDING BLOCKS:
Fruitiness and fattiness with subtle sourness and subtle pleasant bitterness.

FLAVORS:
Ripe berry fruit flavors, black cherry, black raspberries; sometimes with mineral, floral, grassy and spicy characters.

WINES PRODUCED IN THE RED WITH FORWARD FRUIT STYLE

- This is the most popular style of red wine at the moment. Many of the wine regions of the world are producing wines in this fruit-forward style.

- This style of wine has medium to full body.

- Wines in this style can be good quaffers for casual occasions or fine vintages for formal dining. Use them to pair with mini comfort foods or sophisticated appetizers, depending on the depth of character in the accompanying wine.

- Forward fruit means the moment you sip, ripe berry flavors fill your palate. The texture is velvety and there's little to no bitter aftertaste.

- Reds with forward fruit sometimes go through a malolactic fermentation to ensure they possess a soft, creamy texture with little bitterness.

- Due to their moderate tannin, reds with forward fruit can work with gentle heat and spice. Pair caramelized fruit preserves low in sugar with these wines, as well, such as a diabetic raspberry jam on barbecued chicken or ribs.

- Wines in this style also work with mushrooms, bacon and highly fatty cheeses, such as aged cheddar, triple-cream brie, blue cheese and Parmigiano-Reggiano.

The regions below are stylistically noted for producing red wines with forward fruit.

REGIONS

merlot
Australia
Canada (British Columbia, Ontario)
Chile
New Zealand
United States (California)

others
Burgundy — France
Côtes du Rhône-Villages — France
Grenache — Australia
Malbec — France
Shiraz — Australia
Zinfandel — United States (California)

caramelized onion, rosemary & stilton flatbread

My friend Sadie Darby developed this recipe. She's the administrator for the Wine Writers' Circle of Canada and organizes many wine award competitions. She made these flatbreads for us one night; we talked little and moaned a lot! Combining the flavors of sweet caramelized onions, herbaceous fresh rosemary and salty, rich Stilton is truly hedonistic.

Serves 4–6 (makes 18 slices)

2 Tbsp	25 mL	olive oil
6		medium-sized white onions, thinly sliced
		sea salt to taste
3		9-inch (23 cm) whole wheat tortillas
1 Tbsp	15 mL	chopped fresh rosemary
3 oz	90 g	crumbled Stilton
		freshly ground black pepper to taste

Preheat the oven to 400°F (200°C). Heat the oil in a large skillet over medium heat. Add the onions. Stir the onions until they're coated with oil. Season them with salt. (Salt draws the moisture from the onions, helping them to caramelize more quickly.) If the onions stick to the bottom of the pan, add more water if needed, 1 Tbsp (15 mL) at a time. Cook, stirring occasionally, until the natural sugars in the onions caramelize, about 25 minutes. Spread the caramelized onion mixture onto the tortillas. They'll be open-faced. Sprinkle them with the fresh rosemary. Sprinkle the tortillas with the crumbled Stilton. Season them with freshly ground black pepper. Bake the tortillas until they're crisp and the cheese is melted, about 12 minutes. Serve them hot.

building blocks
The predominant building blocks are sweetness from the onions, fruitiness from the rosemary and saltiness from the Stilton. A red with forward fruit has ripe fruit flavors that harmonize with the onions and rosemary and soft to medium bitterness to offset the saltiness in the cheese.

flavors
Choose a red with forward fruit offering earthy flavors to draw out the earthy character of this wonderful blue cheese.

roasted red pepper & white cheddar antojitos with pesto

Montana's Restaurant created a version of this appetizer. I enjoy them so much at our local Montana's that I developed my own healthy version, using multigrain tortillas. Low-fat cream cheese makes these babies even healthier.

Serves 4–6 (makes 12 pinwheels)

8 oz	250 g	cream cheese, at room temperature
½ cup	125 mL	shredded extra-old white cheddar cheese
1		roasted red pepper, diced
1		jalapeño pepper, finely chopped
3		9-inch (23 cm) multigrain tortillas
		pesto (optional)

Preheat the oven to 375°F (190°C). Combine the cream cheese, cheddar cheese, red pepper and jalapeño in a bowl. Divide the mixture evenly into 3 parts. Spread it evenly onto each tortilla. Roll up the tortillas. Place the rolls seam side down on a rimmed baking sheet sprayed with nonstick cooking spray. Bake the tortillas for 5 to 6 minutes, or until golden. Let them cool slightly. Cut the ends of the tortillas on a diagonal, using a sharp knife. Then cut each tortilla into 4 diagonal pinwheels. Serve the tortillas hot or at room temperature with pesto on the side.

building blocks
The predominant building block is fattiness from the cream cheese and cheddar. A red with forward fruit has enough fattiness to match.

flavors
Choose a red with forward fruit and some earth tones to harmonize with the nutty flavor of the white cheddar cheese.

tiny rib lamb chops with rosemary

I first tasted this simple dish when one of my best friends, Cathy Reggeri-Davidson, cooked it for me. She's Southern Italian and loves to cook with simple ingredients in a rustic European style. I was astounded by how fruity the rosemary had become, losing its bitterness when slow-roasted on the lamb. This fruitiness was an orgasmic complement to our glass of Merlot. "Orgasmic" is a term that both Cathy and I love to use to describe wine and food partnerships with heightened appeal.

Serves 4–6 (makes 16 chops)

2		racks of lamb (a total of 2 lb/1 kg)*
½ cup	125 mL	olive oil (for coating)
½ cup	125 mL	finely chopped fresh rosemary
		sea salt to taste
		freshly ground black pepper to taste
		olive oil (for searing and coating roasting pan)

*Buy your lamb chops from a butcher. Ask the butcher to french the chops—that is, to remove as much fat as possible from the ribs and the flesh.

Preheat the oven to 400°F (200°C). Place an empty roasting pan in the oven. Meanwhile, coat the chops in the olive oil. Sprinkle them with the rosemary. Season them with salt and pepper. To prepare the lamb, make sure that all the fat cover and bone fragments have been removed. Add a few drops of oil to a large skillet set on high heat. When the oil is very hot, sear the lamb racks on all sides until they're brown. Remove them from the skillet.

Remove the hot roasting pan from the oven. Add the oil. Put the lamb racks, bone side down, in the hot roasting pan. Roast the lamb for 15 to 20 minutes, to your desired doneness. Then allow the lamb to rest at room temperature for about 10 minutes before cutting it into individual chops. Serve the chops hot.

building blocks
The predominant building blocks are fattiness and fruitiness from the lamb and slow-roasted rosemary. A red with forward fruit has enough fattiness and forward fruitiness to match.

flavors
Choose a red with forward fruit with earthy flavors to harmonize with the gamy nature of lamb.

roast beef & avocado whole wheat sliders with korean mayo

Korean chili, used in the making of kimchi, is a great product with which to work. The chili offers loads of flavor, but with gentle heat and spice. In this appetizer the Korean chili adds flavor to the sliders, without any of the major heat that would normally clash with the bitterness and dryness (tannin and astringency) in red wine.

Serves 4–6
(makes 18 pieces)

¼ cup	50 mL	mayonnaise
1 tsp	5 mL	Korean kimchi chili flakes*
12		slices whole wheat bread
1		ripe avocado
1 Tbsp	15 mL	freshly squeezed lemon juice
1 Tbsp	15 mL	finely chopped fresh chives
		sea salt to taste
		freshly ground black pepper to taste
18		slices deli rare roast beef

*Korean kimchi chili flakes are available at Asian supermarkets.

Purée the mayonnaise and chili flakes in a food processor. Transfer to a bowl. Set the mixture aside. Cut the crusts off the bread slices. Lay a slice on a clean work surface. Flatten the bread slice using a rolling pin. Repeat for all slices.

Mash the avocado with a fork in a bowl. Add the lemon juice and chives. Season the mixture with salt and pepper. Spread the avocado mixture over 6 slices of bread. Spread the other 6 slices of bread with the Korean mayonnaise. Top the mayonnaise-topped slices with 3 slices of roast beef. Gently press each slice of the avocado-topped bread together with a slice of the bread with roast beef on it to make a sandwich. Cut each sandwich into 3 strips using a serrated knife. Cover and chill the sandwiches until they're needed, then bring them to room temperature just before serving them.

building blocks
The predominant building block is fattiness, due to the avocado and mayonnaise. A red with forward fruit has enough fattiness (high alcohol) to match.

flavors
Choose a red with forward fruit offering earthy character to harmonize with the flavor of the roast beef.

sorry, honey, I have a headache!

No one really knows why red wine gives some wine lovers a headache, or, worse, a migraine. Many theories exist as to why this is so. Sulfites, tannins, histamines and tyramines are believed to be the culprits.

Some believe the sulfites in red wine are the primary source. Winemakers use sulfites at various times during the wine-making process. They're used in wine-making for their anti-oxidant and antimicrobial properties.

Contrary to popular belief, red wines do not contain more sulfites than whites. All wines contain sulfites, including whites, reds and particularly sweet wines. In fact, sweet wines require more sulfites than others, due to their sugary content.

A true allergic reaction to sulfites is believed to be quite rare. Here's a simple test to find out if you're allergic to sulfites. Sulfites are found in dried fruits, such as raisins and dried apricots. So, if you experience a headache after eating dried fruit, you may also have an allergic reaction to the sulfites in wine. If you don't experience a headache from dried fruit, you're no doubt reacting to something else in the red wine.

The red wine headache is more likely a reaction to allergens, as they're 20 to 200 percent higher in red wines than in white.

If you take a grape from the vine and rub one of your fingers across its skin, you'll have rubbed something off. This is the bloom, a protective, sticky, water-repellent substance that attaches itself to the grape's skin. Due to its sticky nature, the bloom attracts and grabs onto allergens from the air. Since the skins of grapes are fermented with the juice in the production of red wine, these allergens are also imparted to the mixture. The allergens release histamines in our body.

Today, the skins, stems and pits may also be fermented with the juice in the production of some white wines. So those suffering from allergies may be negatively affected by both red and white wine.

Tyramines may also be the cause. Tyramines are an amino acid found in many foods, such as cheese and chocolate, as well as in robust red wines. Tyramines are believed to cause an increase in blood pressure and thus hyper-tension and a headache.

No doubt the best way to prevent the red wine headache is to refrain from sipping wine made from the red grape.

If you insist, then try experimenting with light, fruity reds. To find a light, fruity red, hold the wine bottle up to a fluorescent light. If you can see light shining through the liquid, then you've found a red fermented in this style. Such reds are fermented with their skins for a shorter period and so tend to possess less tannin and perhaps fewer allergens. So you may be able to sip a light, fruity red wine without experienc-ing an allergic reaction. Gamay is an example of a light, fruity red.

umami jalapeño peppers

The secret of this pub recipe lies in using quality ingredients packed with flavor. Extra-old cheddar cheese, Worcestershire and bacon are all ingredients high in umami and are there-fore highly addictive.

Serves 4–6
(makes 50 pieces)

25		fresh medium-sized jalapeño peppers
4 oz	125 g	cream cheese, softened
1 cup	250 mL	grated extra-old cheddar cheese
½ tsp	2 mL	Worcestershire sauce
1 Tbsp	15 mL	finely chopped fresh parsley
2		slices cooked bacon, crumbled

Preheat the oven to 400°F (200°C). Cut the jalapeño peppers in half lengthwise; remove their seeds. Toss the peppers into a pot of boiling salted water. Blanch them for 5 minutes. Drain them and set them to dry on paper towel. Combine the cream cheese, cheddar cheese, Worcestershire sauce, parsley and bacon in a bowl and mix them together well. Place 1 tsp (5 mL) of the mixture in each pepper shell. Place the jalapeños on a rimmed baking sheet sprayed with nonstick cooking spray. Bake them for 10 minutes, or until the jalapeños are tender and the mixture is melted.

building blocks
The predominant building blocks are fattiness from the cream cheese, cheddar cheese and bacon and heat and spice from the jalapeño peppers. A red with forward fruit has enough fattiness to match. The wine's soft bitterness does not conflict with the gentle heat and spice.

flavors
Choose a red with forward fruit that offers earthy notes to complement the flavor of the cheddar cheese.

spanish chorizo empanadillas

This is a traditional Spanish tapa. I love these little fellas. They're fast and easy to prepare, but have loads of big flavor. A red wine with forward fruit character has soft bitterness (tannin) that won't clash with the spiciness of the chorizo sausage.

Serves 4–6 (makes about 24 empanadillas)

4	chorizo sausages, casings removed
2	sheets puff pastry, thawed
	all-purpose flour for dusting
1	beaten egg, to glaze
	paprika (for garnish)

Preheat the oven to 400°F (200°C). Squeeze the chorizo from its casings. Break up the raw sausage. Roll out the puff pastry on a clean floured work surface. Cut out 24 rounds, using a 2-inch (5 cm) cookie cutter or the rim of a wine glass. Place about 1 tsp (5 mL) of raw chorizo in the middle of each round. Dampen the edges of the dough. Fold the dough over to seal it, using your fingertips. Pull the ends of the dough together and squeeze. Make a small slit with a sharp knife on the top of each empanadilla. Place the empanadillas on a rimmed baking sheet sprayed with nonstick cooking spray. Bake for 10 to 15 minutes, or until the puff pastry is golden. Remove the empanadillas from the oven. Dust the top of each one with paprika. Serve the empanadillas hot.

building blocks
The predominant building block is fattiness, due to the puff pastry and sausage. A red with forward fruit is ideal as its soft bitterness and low tannin won't clash with the spiciness in the sausage.

flavors
Choose a red with forward fruit with earthy notes to harmonize with the flavor of the pork.

spicy 'n smoky two-day, two-bite ribs

One of the participants in my wine course at Fleming College, Ron Walker, gave me the original recipe for his famous ribs. "It's a process, not a recipe," Ron explained. By adding hot sauce to the boiling water, the heat penetrates right into the flesh. This gives the resulting ribs a hot sensation in the after-taste that doesn't interfere with the soft tannin in a red wine with forward fruit flavors. Ron brought his famous ribs to one of our food and wine pairing classes. We all moaned in delight and finished every last rib. I knew this "process" had to be in this cookbook. Because they're so messy, these ribs are best suited for a casual affair.

Serves 4–6

6–8 cups	1.5–2 L	Dr. Pepper soda pop
2		racks of baby back ribs* (a total of 4 lb/2 kg)
¼ cup	50 mL	hot sauce
¾ cup	175 mL	Montreal Steak Spice
1 cup	250 mL	mesquite-flavored barbecue sauce (of choice)

*Have the butcher remove the membrane from the back of the ribs.

Pour the Dr. Pepper into a large pot, covering the ribs completely. Add the hot sauce. Boil the ribs over high heat until the liquid turns clear, about 40 minutes. Remove the ribs from the liquid and set them on paper towel to drain. Sprinkle a cutting board with Montreal Steak Spice. Roll the ribs in the spice, coating them well all over. Set the coated ribs on a rimmed baking sheet, cover them and refrigerate them overnight.

When you're ready to barbecue, coat the ribs completely with the sauce. Position them over indirect heat on the grill, skin side down. Grill the ribs, turning them occasionally to heat them through. Increase the heat for the last few minutes to caramelize the sauce. Set the racks on a clean cutting board and cut them into individual ribs. Serve them hot. (You'll need extra napkins.)

building blocks
The predominant building blocks are fattiness from the meat and some sweetness from the barbecue sauce. A red with forward fruit has the fattiness to stand up to the weight and texture of ribs. The wine's fruitiness but low bitterness and astringency (tannin) don't clash with the heat and sweetness in this recipe.

flavors
Choose a red with forward fruit offering earthy tones to harmonize with the smoky flavors of mesquite sauce.

wild mushroom & brie bruschetta

I created this recipe to serve to a dear friend and major foodie, Judy Creighton. I wanted Judy to experience how the Building Block Principles found on my learning tool called the Canadian Food and Wine Pairing Wheel worked, not just intellectually, but experientially. I waited anxiously for her response. When she started to moan, I knew I had developed another recipe for my next cookbook.

Serves 4–6 (makes 12 slices)

12		slices whole wheat bread
3–4		cloves garlic, minced
½ cup	125 mL	olive oil
¼ cup	50 mL	butter
1½ cups	375 mL	chopped shiitake mushrooms
¼ cup	50 mL	finely chopped fresh basil
		sea salt to taste
		freshly ground black pepper to taste
1¼ lb	625 g	ripened French brie, thinly sliced*

*Be sure to check the brie's wrapping to ensure it's stabilizer free. The stabilizer will keep the brie from ripening in flavor. This is important if you're a nontaster and cherish the earthy flavors of ripened brie.

Preheat the broiler. Under the broiler, grill 1 side of each bread slice until it's golden, 1 to 2 minutes. Rub the toasted sides with a raw garlic clove. Drizzle each slice with olive oil. In a skillet, melt the butter over low heat. Lightly sauté the mushrooms until they're tender, about 5 minutes. Remove the skillet from the heat. Fold in the basil and season with salt and pepper. Place the mushroom mixture on the oiled side of the toasts. Lay the brie slices on top of the mushroom mixture. Grill the bruschetta slices under the broiler until the cheese begins to run. Place the bruschetta slices on warm plates and serve them immediately.

building blocks
The predominant building block of this appetizer is fattiness in the olive oil, butter and brie. A red with forward fruit has enough fattiness to match.

flavors
Choose a red with forward fruit and earthy flavors to complement the earthy taste of the brie and wild mushrooms.

peking duck gow gee with soy dipping sauce

Gow gee *is the Cantonese name for steamed or deep-fried dumplings. While you can make the skins yourself, wonton wrappers are an acceptable substitute and are readily available in supermarkets. These dumplings are wonderfully orgasmic, due to the umami in the mushrooms, hoisin and soy sauce.*

Serves 4–6 (makes 12–14 dumplings)

Dipping sauce:

1 Tbsp	15 mL	light soy sauce
1 Tbsp	15 mL	rice vinegar
½ tsp	2 mL	sesame oil

Gow gee:

1 Tbsp	15 mL	sesame oil
¼ cup	50 mL	diced shiitake mushrooms
½ cup	125 mL	diced cooked duck (or chicken) meat
¼ cup	50 mL	diced green onions
2 Tbsp	25 mL	hoisin
2 tsp	10 mL	light Chinese soy sauce
12–14		wonton wrappers
		sea salt to taste
		freshly ground black pepper to taste
		water (as needed)

Combine the dipping sauce ingredients in a small bowl. Cover it and refrigerate it until it's needed.

To make the gow gee, heat the oil in a large skillet over medium heat. Add the mushrooms. Sauté the mushrooms until they're tender, about 3 minutes. Remove the skillet from the heat and set it aside. Combine the mushrooms, duck meat, onions, hoisin and soy sauce in a large bowl and mix them together well.

Lay the wonton wrappers out on a flat surface. Place 1 tsp (5 mL) of mixture in the center of each wonton wrapper. Dip your fingers in water and moisten the edges of each wrapper. Fold the wrappers in half to form half-circles. Pinch in the center of each half-circle. Pinch together the right corner and then pinch together the dough between the corner and the middle. Repeat on the other side. Seal whatever gaps remain so the dumpling is completely sealed. The dumpling will sit up in a slightly curved shape. Be sure no meat is hanging out of the seam.

Spray a bamboo steamer with nonstick cooking spray. Fill the steamer with dumplings. Place the steamer in a skillet filled with 1 inch (2.5 cm) of water. Steam the dumplings on high heat for 3 to 4 minutes, until tender. Repeat the process until all the dumplings are steamed. Serve them hot with dipping sauce.

building blocks

The primary building blocks are fattiness due to the duck and sesame oil, saltiness due to the soy sauce and a hint of sweetness from the hoisin. A red wine with forward fruit harmonizes with the fattiness and salt. And the forward fruit and low bitterness and astringency works with the hoisin's subtle sweetness.

flavors

Choose a red with forward fruit character and earthy tones to bring out the subtle flavor of the shiitake mushrooms.

cambozola & toasted walnut pâté

If you're entertaining a large group of people, it's smart to pick a few appetizers you can make ahead of time. This is certainly one of them. Overnight the flavors of the cheese, rosemary and walnuts meld together and taste fabulous with a red wine.

Serves 4–6

8 oz	250 g	Cambozola
4 oz	125 g	cream cheese
½ cup	125 mL	butter
2 Tbsp	25 mL	sour cream
½ tsp	2 mL	finely chopped fresh rosemary
½ cup	125 mL	toasted walnuts*
		freshly ground black pepper to taste
		sprig of rosemary (for garnish)
1		baguette

*Walnuts can be toasted in a dry skillet over medium heat, tossing them frequently, for about 3 minutes.

Combine the Cambozola, cream cheese and butter in a food processor or blender and mix them together until they're smooth. Transfer the mixture to a serving bowl. Fold in the sour cream, rosemary and walnuts. Season the mixture to taste with black pepper. Cover it and refrigerate it until it's needed. Before serving, garnish the bowl with the rosemary sprig and serve the pâté with slices of baguette.

building blocks
The predominant building blocks are fattiness and saltiness from the Cambozola and butter. A red with forward fruit has enough fattiness to match. The wine's soft bitterness and astringency (tannins) nicely offset the saltiness.

flavors
Choose a red with forward fruit offering earthy flavors to match the earthy flavor of the Cambozola.

mini red potato skins stuffed with chorizo & parmesan

If you look at a recipe and see three or more umami-rich ingredients, you know you've got tiny bites with the MOAN FACTOR. Potatoes, chorizo sausage, Parmigiano-Reggiano and olives are a celebration of this fifth taste sensation.

Serves 4–6 (makes 36 mini potato skins)

18		variety of mini potatoes
3 Tbsp	40 mL	olive oil
½ tsp	2 mL	sea salt
¾ cup	175 mL	finely diced chorizo meat, removed from sausage casings
½ cup	125 mL	finely chopped onion
3		cloves garlic, minced
¼ cup	50 mL	dried breadcrumbs
¾ cup	175 mL	freshly grated Parmigiano-Reggiano
10		pimento-stuffed olives, finely chopped
		sea salt to taste
		freshly ground black pepper to taste

building blocks
The predominant building blocks are heat and spice from the chorizo, saltiness from the Parmigiano-Reggiano and bitterness from the olives. A red wine with forward fruit won't clash with the heat and spice and will complement the hint of saltiness and bitterness.

flavors
Choose a red with forward fruit offering earthy character to complement the depth of flavor in the chorizo sausage.

Preheat the oven to 400°F (200°C). Cut the potatoes in half. Cut a little slice off the bottom of each half potato so it will sit flat. Using a melon-baller, cut out each potato's flesh, leaving a ¼-inch-thick (5 mm) shell. Discard the raw potato. Toss the skins with olive oil and sea salt. Arrange the skins on a rimmed baking sheet sprayed with nonstick cooking spray. Bake them for 15 minutes, or until they're tender. Turn the shells over and bake them for another 10 minutes, until they're golden and crisp. Remove them from the heat. Set them aside.

Cook the chorizo in a skillet over medium heat until it's browned, about 5 minutes. Remove the meat with a slotted spoon and drain it on paper towel. Add the onion to the pan and cook it until it's translucent, about 5 minutes. Add the garlic and cook the mixture for another minute. Stir in the chorizo, breadcrumbs, Parmigiano and olives. Season the mixture to taste with salt and pepper. Spoon it into the baked shells and mound it neatly. Bake the potato skins for 10 minutes, or until they're heated through. Serve them hot.

tickle my ribs

When serving ribs as an appetizer, I prefer to use a dry rub rather than using sauce. Ribs with sauce can be too messy, especially when your guests are also holding a glass of wine. Ribs with sauce are better suited for casual affairs and less appropriate for more formal gatherings. Here's a recipe using my own commercial dry rub called Tickle My Ribs.

Serves 4–6

2		racks of baby back ribs*
		olive oil (as needed)
¼ lb	230 g	Orgasmic Culinary Creations Tickle My Ribs dry rub (½ bag)**

*Have the butcher remove the membrane from the back of the ribs.

**Turn to the last page for more details on how to purchase Tickle My Ribs. Or substitute with homemade All-Purpose Dry Rub (see page 219).

Preheat the oven to 250°F (120°C). Trim the excess fat from the ribs. Place the ribs on a large plate. Coat the ribs in olive oil. Generously coat the ribs with Tickle My Ribs dry rub. Pat the dry rub into the ribs. Cover the ribs with plastic wrap. Place the ribs on a greased, rimmed baking sheet. Slow-roast the ribs for 4 hours. Remove them from the oven. Turn off the heat. Wrap them in foil. Set the foiled ribs back in the oven. Leave the oven door slightly ajar. Let the ribs rest in the oven for ½ hour. Set the racks on a clean cutting board and cut them into individual ribs. Serve them hot.

building blocks
The predominant building blocks are fattiness from the meat and heat and spice, bitterness, sweetness and saltiness from the dry rub. A red with forward fruit has soft tannin, which does not clash with the multiple flavors in the ribs.

flavors
Choose a red with forward fruit offering ripe blackberry tones to match the sweetness in the dry rub.

lamb chops with mint chili chutney

Buy your lamb chops from a butcher. Ask the butcher to french the chops, to remove as much fat as possible from the ribs and flesh.

*Serves 4–6
(makes 16 chops)*

2 tsp	10 mL	curry powder
2 Tbsp	25 mL	finely chopped fresh cilantro
2 Tbsp	25 mL	minced garlic
		sea salt to taste
		freshly ground black pepper to taste
2		racks of lamb (a total of 2 lb/1 kg)
		olive oil (for searing and coating the roasting pan)

Chutney:

1 cup	250 mL	fresh mint leaves
½ cup	125 mL	chopped green onion
1 Tbsp	15 mL	sugar
½		fresh Thai or Asian hot green chili, minced
2 Tbsp	25 mL	rice vinegar
		sea salt to taste
		freshly ground black pepper to taste
		olive oil (as needed)

building blocks
The predominant building blocks are fattiness from the lamb and gentle heat and spice from the curry powder and Thai chili. A red with forward fruit has enough fat to match, while its forward fruit and gentle bitterness don't clash with the heat and spice.

flavors
Choose a red with forward fruit with some herbal tones to match the flavor of the mint.

In a food processor or blender, combine the curry powder, cilantro, garlic, salt and pepper. Rub the mixture on both sides of the lamb; cover and refrigerate it for 24 hours.

Preheat the oven to 400°F (200°C). Place an empty roasting pan in the oven. Combine the chutney ingredients in a food processor or blender and blend them well.

Add a few drops of oil to a large skillet and heat it on high until it's very hot. Sear the lamb racks on all sides until they're brown. Pull the empty pan from the oven. Add the oil. Place the lamb racks, bone side down, in the hot pan. Roast them for 15 to 20 minutes, to the desired doneness. Allow the lamb to rest at room temperature for about 10 minutes, then cut it into individual chops. Place each chop on a small plate and garnish it with 1 Tbsp (15 mL) of the chutney.

orgasmic appetizers to pair with austere reds

Austere reds

PREDOMINANT BUILDING BLOCKS:
Fattiness and pleasant bitterness and dryness with subtle fruitiness and sourness.

Aged versions can also offer the fifth taste sensation of umami.

FLAVORS:
Smoky, earthy, woody, coffee, chocolatey, leathery, tobacco, blueberry, blackberry, raspberry, blackcurrant, cassis, tea, eucalyptus.

WINES PRODUCED IN THE AUSTERE RED STYLE

- Austere reds, due to their bitterness and dryness (tannin and astringency) when balanced with their fruit and acidity, have great aging potential.

- These reds are generally medium- to full-bodied with high alcohol.

- Barrel fermentation and barrel aging are generally employed to help add complexity, flavor and structure.

- Due to their high alcohol content, austere reds work well with fatty foods, such as goose, duck, beef, lamb and foie gras. High-fat cheeses are also an excellent match, including Parmigiano-Reggiano, hard and soft blue cheeses, very ripe brie and extra-old cheddar cheese.

- Winter vegetables have enough weight for austere reds. This includes potatoes, carrots and eggplant.

- Earthy versions work nicely with ripened cheeses like brie, as well as with wild mushrooms and black and white truffles.

- Their backbone of pleasant bitterness also makes them an ideal partner for salty foods, such as aged cheeses.

- Austere reds also work with bitter foods, such as spinach, olives and radicchio. These lighter foods must be combined with heavier ingredients to stand up to the weight of an austere red wine.

The regions below are stylistically noted for producing austere reds.

REGIONS

cabernet sauvignon
Chile
South Africa
United States (California)

others
Baco Noir — Canada (Ontario), France
Barbaresco — Italy (Piedmont)
Barolo — Italy (Piedmont)
Haut-Médoc — France (Bordeaux)
Margaux — France (Bordeaux)
Pauillac — France (Bordeaux)
Pinotage — South Africa
Saint-Estèphe — France (Bordeaux)
Saint-Julien — France (Bordeaux)
Shiraz — Australia

truffle mashed potatoes with garlic & caramelized leeks

The truffle oil in these mashed potatoes adds another layer of umami-rich flavor, along with the other complex flavors. This small addition to an otherwise simple comfort food also acts like a bridge, fusing all the flavors together. To serve them as an appetizer, use Chinese spoons.

Serves 4–6
(makes 24 bite-sized servings)

¼ cup	50 mL	butter
6		garlic cloves, coarsely chopped
3		leeks (white parts only), halved lengthwise
1 tsp	5 mL	sugar dissolved in 1 tsp (5 mL) water
		sea salt to taste
		freshly ground black pepper to taste
1½ lb	750 g	russet potatoes, peeled, cut into 1-inch (2.5 cm) pieces
¼ cup	50 mL	half and half cream (more if needed)
½ cup	125 mL	mascarpone cheese
2 Tbsp	25 mL	black truffle oil*
		sea salt to taste
		freshly ground black pepper to taste

*Black truffle oil is available in most gourmet retail shops.

Melt the butter in a skillet over medium heat. Add the garlic and sauté it until it's aromatic. Add the leeks and sugar water. Stir the mixture to coat the leeks in butter. Cook it until the leeks are golden brown, stirring them every 5 minutes, about 20 minutes. Season them to taste with salt and pepper.

Meanwhile, cook the potatoes in a large pot of boiling salted water until they're tender, about 25 minutes. Drain them well. Put the potatoes through a potato ricer into the pot in which they were boiled. Add the cream, mascarpone and truffle oil and fold them together. Do not overmix. Season them with salt and pepper. Place a spoonful of mashed potato in each Chinese spoon and top it with the leek mixture. Serve the potatoes hot.

building blocks
The predominant building block is fattiness, due to the butter and cream. An austere red has enough weight to match.

flavors
Choose an austere red with flavors of barnyard and wet soil to complement the similar characteristics in truffle oil.

yummy mini marinated beef skewers

This is a simple recipe that shows how the combination of a few umami-rich ingredients can do the trick to transform tasty beef skewers into an appetizer with the MOAN FACTOR.

Serves 4–6
(makes 18 skewers)

1 lb	500 g	aged beef (top round)
2 Tbsp	25 mL	light Chinese soy sauce
1 Tbsp	15 mL	dry sherry
1 tsp	5 mL	sesame oil
3		cloves garlic, minced
18		bamboo skewers (6 inch/15 cm), soaked overnight in water (soak some extras just in case; they're cheap)

Cut the beef crosswise into 18 slices (⅛ inch/3 mm) thick. Place them in a bowl. Combine the soy sauce, sherry, oil and garlic in another bowl. Mix them together well. Pour the mixture over the beef and toss the beef in it. Cover the bowl and refrigerate it for 2 hours. Preheat the grill. Drain the beef. Discard the marinade. Weave the beef accordion-style along the skewers. Position the skewers on the barbecue grill and grill them for 2 minutes per side, or until the beef is done to your liking.

building blocks
The predominant building blocks are fattiness and saltiness from the soy sauce. An austere red has enough bitterness to offset the saltiness.

flavors
Choose an austere red with earthy character to harmonize with the umami-rich taste of these skewers.

stuffed olives with gorgonzola

Stuffed olives fall more into the category of nibbles than actual appetizers. Put these olives in colorful bowls on side tables around the room.

Serves 4–6 (makes 24 stuffed olives)

1 oz	30 g	Gorgonzola
24		pitted Spanish olives, patted dry
		peanut oil (for deep-frying)
		all-purpose flour (for dredging)
1		large egg, beaten to blend
½ cup	125 mL	fine dried breadcrumbs
		toothpicks

Roll a small amount of the Gorgonzola into a log shape narrow enough to stuff into 1 pitted olive; stuff the olive with the cheese. Repeat with the remaining olives and cheese. Set them in a bowl, cover it and refrigerate it overnight.

Pour enough oil into a large, heavy skillet for deep-frying. Heat the oil to 375°F (190°C). Roll the stuffed olives in the flour, then in the egg, then in the breadcrumbs to coat. Fry the olives until they're golden brown, about 30 seconds. Using a slotted spoon, transfer the olives to paper towels to drain. Serve them hot or at room temperature with toothpicks.

building blocks
The predominant building block is bitterness from the olives. An austere red with bitterness is the best match.

flavors
Choose an austere red with earthy flavors to harmonize with the earthiness of the Gorgonzola.

mini crisp potato skins with brie & bacon

Chef Steve Benns is a professor in the culinary division at Fleming College. Chef Steve does a great deal of catering for family and friends. This is one of the appetizers that people ask him to prepare time and time again.

Serves 4–6 (makes 24 mini potato skins)

12		mini red potatoes
		corn oil (for deep-frying)
8		slices double-smoked bacon, diced
6		green onions, diced
3		cloves garlic, minced
12		sprigs fresh thyme, stems removed, leaves finely chopped
		sea salt to taste
		freshly ground black pepper to taste
3½ oz	105 g	ripened French brie

Wash the potatoes. Cut a thin slice off the top and bottom of each potato to make a flat surface for it to sit on. Cut the potato in half, parallel to the first 2 cuts. Using a melon baller or paring knife, scoop out the inside, leaving about ¼ inch (5 mm) of potato with the skin. Put the potatoes into a large pot of cold water. Bring the water to a boil. Add salt. Cook the potatoes for 15 minutes, or until just before tender. Remove the potatoes from the pot using a slotted spoon. Transfer the potatoes to a cool water bath. Heat the oil to 375°F (190°C) in a large pot. Deep-fry the potato skins for 2 to 3 minutes, or until they're golden brown. Remove the skins using a slotted spoon. Let them cool.

Preheat the oven to 375°F (190°C). Sauté the bacon in a large skillet until it's almost cooked. Add the green onions, garlic and thyme. Sauté the mixture for 2 minutes, or until it's aromatic. Season it with salt and pepper. Chop the brie into small pieces and place it in each hollowed-out skin. Place about 1 oz (30 g) of the onion mixture on top of the brie. Place the potato skins on a rimmed baking sheet sprayed with nonstick cooking spray. Grill them for 10 minutes, or until the cheese is melted and the skins are hot. Serve hot or at room temperature.

---

building blocks
The predominant building block is fattiness due to the bacon and brie. An austere red has enough fattiness to match.

flavors
Choose an austere red with toasty, smoky tones to harmonize with the flavor of the bacon.

decanting is romantic!

Decanting is ritualistic and therefore adds ambience and romance to every occasion. Whites are generally meant to be consumed within the first two years of purchase and therefore don't require decanting. However, some people prefer to decant big white wines. This is often done to aerate them and open up their aromas.

Decanting is the process of transferring wine from its bottle into a decanter. A decanter can be a glass pitcher or a carafe. Its purpose is three-fold. Decanting is necessary when a young wine needs aeration, an old vintage has deposited some sediment in the bottom of the bottle or cork parts have slipped into the bottle.

The best decanters for young wines look similar to a science beaker. This decanter is narrow at the top with a wide, almost flat base. The wider base allows for more of the surface of the wine to be exposed to the air and therefore aerate more readily. Adding air to a young wine helps open up the aromas and helps soften some of the bitter bite from its youthful tannins.

Putting an opened bottle of wine on the table doesn't help it breathe, as decanting does. In that case, the only wine that's exposed to air and can therefore breathe is the small surface inside the bottleneck. The point is to allow as much wine as possible to be exposed to the air.

When decanting young wines, remove the foil from the bottleneck and pull the cork. Tip the bottle into the decanter at a 90-degree angle. The angle allows the wine to tumble aggressively into the decanter. This tumbling action pulls in air, helping to aerate the wine. Let the wine sit in a cool place for a couple of hours before serving.

Narrow decanters are ideal for extremely old reds. Old reds don't necessarily need to have their tannins softened. Decanting is primarily used to remove the sediment from a wine. The sediment in the bottle accumulates over time. This takes place when the wine is "sleeping" in the wine cellar. Sediment is made up of dead yeast, color pigments and tannin that slowly precipitate to the bottom of the bottle over the years. Sediment can be displeasing to the eyes and taste buds.

To decant older wines, remove the foil from the bottleneck. Gently remove the cork from the wine. In old vintages, the cork may be brittle or dry, causing it to split or break off into pieces. Uncork the wine. Clean the neck and inside lip of the bottle with a damp cloth. The idea is not to allow any dust or cork to fall into the bottle.

Light a candle and sit it in a candleholder. Hold the wine bottle in one hand and the decanter in the other. Position the bottle well above and just in front of the flame; do not let the candle heat the wine. Tilt the decanter slightly. The candle will illuminate the bottleneck, allowing you to see sediment climbing toward the bottleneck. Continue to steadily pour the wine into the decanter until the sediment reaches the bottleneck. Save the bottle. Your guests may want to look at the label. Serve the wine from the decanter. Decanting old wines can be done in advance or at the table as you dine. It's a beautiful ritual that adds to the experience of celebrating with loved ones, lovers and friends.

polenta rounds with stilton pâté

You'll need to make the polenta rounds from cornmeal. The prepared polenta tubes available at supermarkets won't work here; the rounds made from those tubes are too large to serve as bite-sized morsels. The ready-made polenta also can't be punched with a cookie cutter.

*Serves 4–6
(makes 16 rounds)*

building blocks
The predominant building block is fattiness and saltiness from the Stilton. An austere red has enough tannin to nicely offset the fat and salt in Stilton.

flavors
Choose an austere red with berry flavors to complement the piquant flavor of Stilton.

Pâté:

8 oz	250 g	cream cheese
4 oz	125 g	crumbled Stilton
2		cloves minced garlic
1 tsp	5 mL	finely chopped fresh rosemary

Polenta:

1 cup	250 mL	milk
½ cup	125 mL	fine cornmeal
		sea salt to taste
		freshly ground black pepper to taste
		corn oil (for frying)
		rosemary sprigs (for garnish)

To make the pâté, combine the cream cheese and Stilton in a bowl. Mix them together until they're well blended. Mix in the garlic and fresh rosemary. Cover the mixture and refrigerate it until it's needed.

To make the polenta, bring the milk almost to the boil. Add the cornmeal in a very slow stream, stirring constantly. Reduce the heat to low. Continue stirring in the same direction while the cornmeal thickens, about 15 to 20 minutes. The polenta is done when it peels easily off the sides of the pot. Season it with salt and pepper. Remove it from the heat. Pour the polenta onto a sheet of aluminum foil. With wet hands, smooth it into a thin, even sheet. Let the polenta cool. Cut out 16 rounds, using a 2-inch (5 cm) cookie cutter or the rim of a wine glass. (Fancy cookie cutters work nicely, too.)

Preheat the oven to 350°F (180°C). Heat the oil in a large skillet over medium heat. Fry the polenta for about 2 minutes on each side, until lightly golden. Meanwhile, spray a rimmed baking sheet with nonstick cooking spray. Set the fried rounds on the baking sheet. Top each round with 1 tsp (5 mL) Stilton pâté. Place the baking sheet in the oven and bake the rounds until the cheese is melted, 3 to 5 minutes. Watch closely so the pâté just melts, but doesn't slide off the polenta. Garnish the rounds with the rosemary sprigs. Serve them warm.

shiitake mushroom & toasted cashew pâté

⅓ cup	75 mL	butter
½ cup	125 mL	green onions (white part only)
1¼ lb	625 g	shiitake mushrooms, thickly sliced
2		cloves garlic, finely chopped
2 tsp	10 mL	curry powder
½ tsp	2 mL	ground cumin
1 cup	250 mL	toasted unsalted cashews*
¼ cup	50 mL	olive oil
		sea salt to taste
		freshly ground black pepper to taste
2 Tbsp	25 mL	finely chopped fresh basil
2 tsp	10 mL	finely grated lemon zest
1		baguette, frozen
		corn oil (for frying)
		sea salt to taste

*Cashews can be toasted in a dry skillet over medium heat, tossing them frequently, for about 3 minutes.

Heat the butter in a skillet on high heat. Add the green onions, mushrooms, garlic, curry and cumin. Sauté the mixture until it's just beginning to brown and the liquid evaporates, about 5 minutes.

Meanwhile, chop the cashews in a food processor or blender. Add the oil and continue to process the nuts into a smooth paste. Add the mushroom mixture to the blender and process the mixture until it's smooth. Season it with salt and pepper. Pour the mixture into a dip dish. Cover and refrigerate it until it's needed.

Just before serving, warm the pâté to room temperature. Sprinkle it with the fresh basil and lemon zest. Slice the frozen baguette, as thinly as possible, into 24 slices, using a sharp serrated knife. Heat the oil until very hot but not smoking in a large skillet. Fry the bread slices until they're golden brown and transfer them to a plate lined with paper towel. Season the toasts with salt. Serve the pâté with the toasts.

building blocks
The predominant building block is fattiness, due to the oil and fattiness in the nuts. An austere red has enough fattiness to match.

flavors
Choose an austere red with earthy notes to harmonize with the earthiness of mushrooms.

wild mushroom & three-cheese bruschetta

While hosting client appreciation events, I often work with a catering company called Appetizers and More, located in the historical and quaint hamlet of Unionville, Ontario. The owner and caterer is Chef Anne Kaukonen. Chef Anne offers a wide variety of appetizers to her clients. And yet, returning clients always request her wild mushroom and three-cheese bruschetta. It's simple and simply delicious.

Serves 4–6 (makes 12 bruschetta)

1		baguette
		olive oil (as needed)
1 Tbsp	15 mL	butter
2 cups	500 mL	chopped assorted wild mushrooms
4 oz	125 g	Gorgonzola
		freshly ground black pepper to taste.
4 oz	125 g	freshly grated Asiago cheese
4 oz	125 g	grated fontina cheese

Preheat the oven to 350°F (180°C). Cut the baguette into 12 slices, about ¼ inch (5 mm) in width. Coat the slices with olive oil and set them aside. In a large skillet over medium heat, heat the butter. Add the wild mushrooms. Sauté them until they're tender, 5 to 7 minutes. Remove them from the heat. Combine the mushrooms and Gorgonzola in a bowl. Season the mixture with pepper. Mix it together well. Spread about 1 Tbsp (15 mL) of the mushroom mixture on each slice of baguette.

Combine the Asiago and fontina in another bowl. Place about 1 Tbsp (15 mL) of the cheese mixture on top of the mushroom mixture. Repeat for all the slices. Place the bruschetta on a rimmed baking sheet sprayed with nonstick cooking spray. Bake for 7 to 10 minutes, or until the slices are golden and the cheeses have melted.

building blocks
The predominant building blocks are fattiness and saltiness from the three cheeses. An austere red has enough fattiness to match and bitterness to offset the saltiness.

flavors
Choose an austere red with earthy aromas to complement the earthiness in the wild mushrooms.

pecan pesto & sun-dried tomato toasts

This is another appetizer I tested on the participants in my Fleming College wine class. It received a definite "yes" because it possesses the MOAN FACTOR.

Serves 4–6 (makes 18 toasts)

36		sun-dried tomatoes*
1 cup	250 mL	fresh basil leaves
½ cup	125 mL	pecan pieces
½ cup	125 mL	extra virgin olive oil
4		cloves garlic
1		baguette, thinly sliced (18 pieces)
¾ cup	175 mL	freshly grated Parmigiano-Reggiano (thick shavings)

*Place the sun-dried tomato strips in olive oil, just enough to cover them. Cover the mixture and refrigerate it overnight.

Preheat the broiler. Drain the sun-dried tomato strips on paper towel. Set them aside. To make the pesto, combine the basil, pecans, oil and garlic in a food processor or blender. Blend them together until they're smooth. Place 18 slices of bread on a rimmed baking sheet sprayed with nonstick cooking spray. Broil them until they're golden, 1 to 2 minutes. Watch closely, being careful not to burn them. Turn and grill the other sides. Remove them from the oven and let them cool.

Spread the pesto evenly over the toasts. Top each with 2 strips of sun-dried tomato. Place the Parmigiano-Reggiano shavings on top. Serve the toasts warm or at room temperature.

building blocks
The predominant building blocks are fattiness from the olive oil, bitterness from the pesto and saltiness from the Parmigiano. An austere red has enough fattiness and bitterness to match. Its bitterness also harmonizes with the saltiness in the Parmigiano.

flavors
Choose a red with blackberry fruit flavor to harmonize with the fruitiness of sun-dried tomatoes.

walnut-coated lamb chops

The skin of walnuts possesses tannin and astringency, acting as a bridge of flavor between the lamb and the wine. Lamb also possesses enough weight to pair with a wine in this austere style.

Serves 4–6 (makes 16 chops)

2		racks of lamb (a total of 2 lb/1 kg)*
½ cup	125 mL	coarsely chopped walnuts
¼ cup	50 mL	flat-leaf parsley leaves
¼ cup	50 mL	fine breadcrumbs
1 Tbsp	15 mL	finely chopped fresh rosemary
2		medium cloves garlic, minced
		sea salt to taste
		freshly ground black pepper to taste
2 Tbsp	25 mL	Dijon mustard
		olive oil (for searing and coating the roasting pan)

* Buy your lamb chops from a butcher. Ask the butcher to french the chops, to remove as much fat as possible from the ribs and flesh.

Preheat the oven to 350°F (180°C). Place an empty roasting pan in the oven. Trim the excess fat from the lamb chops. Combine the walnuts, parsley, breadcrumbs, rosemary, garlic, salt and pepper in a food processor or blender and process them until they're finely ground. Transfer the mixture to a plate. Rub each chop with mustard, then place it in the walnut mixture, turning to coat all sides. Put a few drops of oil in a large skillet and heat it until it's very hot. Sear the lamb racks on all sides, until they're brown. Pull the pan from the oven. Add the oil. Place the lamb racks, bone side down, in the hot roasting pan. Roast them for 15 to 20 minutes, to the desired doneness. Allow the lamb to rest at room temperature for about 10 minutes, then cut it into individual chops. Serve the lamb chops hot.

building blocks
The predominant building blocks are fattiness from the lamb and bitterness from the walnuts and rosemary. An austere red with good bitterness and astringency is a good match.

flavors
Choose an austere red with strong earthy flavors to match the gamy nature of the lamb.

escargot-stuffed mushroom caps with garlic butter & two cheeses

I love the strong, exotic flavor of escargot. This recipe also works nicely with a big, fat white and a red with forward fruit.

Serves 4–6 (makes 12 mushroom caps)

24		small snails, from a can

Garlic butter:

3 Tbsp	40 mL	butter
¼		small onion, finely chopped
2–3		cloves garlic, finely chopped
3 Tbsp	40 mL	finely chopped fresh parsley
		sea salt to taste
		freshly ground black pepper to taste
2 Tbsp	25 mL	butter
12		medium-sized mushroom caps
¼ cup	50 mL	freshly grated Parmigiano-Reggiano
¼ cup	50 mL	shredded mozzarella

building blocks
The predominant building block is fattiness from the butter and cheese. An austere red has enough fattiness to match.

flavors
Choose a red with less fruit, but more leather, tobacco and earthy character to match the earthy flavor of the mushrooms.

Preheat the oven to 450°F (230°C). Rinse the snails and drain them on paper towel. Set them aside. Combine the butter, onion, garlic, parsley, salt and pepper in a food processor or blender. Blend them together until they're smooth. Set aside.

Place 2 Tbsp (25 mL) butter in a large skillet and melt it over medium heat. Sauté the mushroom caps until they're cooked, but still firm. Remove the caps from the skillet and drain them on paper towel. Spray the muffin tin with nonstick cooking spray. Set 1 mushroom cap, cavity facing upward, in each hole of the muffin tin. Place a dollop of garlic butter in the cavity of each mushroom. Press 2 small snails into the garlic butter.

Combine the 2 cheeses in a bowl. (If the grated pieces of cheese are too long, first chop them finely.) Place a generous pinch of the cheese mixture on top of each mushroom cap, over the snails. Place the muffin tin in the oven and cook the mushroom caps for 5 to 7 minutes or until the cheese mixture is melted and bubbling. Serve them hot.

cedar-planked bloomy rind cheese with pesto

Cedar-planking adds a whole dimension of flavor to a variety of appetizers.

Serves 4–6

1		cedar plank, soaked in cold water for 2 to 3 hours
2 Tbsp	25 mL	pesto
1		bloomy rind cheese of choice (about 8 oz/250 g)*
		toasted baguette slices

*Ripe brie is always a safe bet. Just be sure the bloomy rind cheese you choose has loads of earthy flavor, such as Camembert or Cambozola.

Preheat the barbecue. Remove the plank from the water. Spread the pesto on top of the brie. Set the cheese on the plank. Set the plank on the barbecue grill. Close the barbecue lid so the plank begins to smoke. Grill the cheese for about 7 minutes. Watch the cheese carefully so that it softens, but doesn't collapse from the heat. Serve the cedar-planked brie warm, on its singed plank, with toasts.

building blocks
The predominant building block is fattiness from the cheese and pesto. Choose an austere red with enough fattiness to match.

flavors
Choose an austere red with earthy flavors to match the earthy character of a ripe bloomy rind cheese.

mini cheddar & rosemary knishes

Since this is an easy but time-consuming recipe, I suggest you make the filling in advance, cover it and refrigerate it. That will also provide time for the flavors to fuse in the filling. The knishes are delicious hot or at room temperature.

Serves 4–6 (makes 16 knishes)

Dough:

2 cups	500 mL	all-purpose flour
½ tsp	2 mL	sea salt
1		egg
½ cup	125 mL	water
¼ cup	50 mL	vegetable oil
1 tsp	5 mL	white vinegar

Filling:

1 Tbsp	15 mL	butter
2 Tbsp	25 mL	vegetable oil
1		large onion, chopped
1 cup	250 mL	mashed potatoes
1 cup	250 mL	shredded extra-old cheddar cheese
¼ cup	50 mL	cottage cheese
2 Tbsp	25 mL	finely chopped fresh rosemary
		sea salt to taste
		freshly ground black pepper to taste
2 Tbsp	25 mL	olive oil for brushing over the knishes

To make the dough, combine the flour and salt in a large bowl. Make a well in the middle of the flour. Add the egg, water, oil and vinegar. Stirring, mix the ingredients to form a dough. Knead the dough on a clean work surface until it's smooth, about 5 minutes. Cover it with plastic wrap and let it rest for 20 minutes.

Melt the butter in a large skillet over low heat. Add the oil and onion. Cook the onion until it's soft and golden, about 15 minutes. Add a touch of water if necessary.

Combine the onion, mashed potatoes, cheddar cheese, cottage cheese and rosemary in a large bowl. Season the filling with salt and pepper.

Preheat the oven to 375°F (190°C). Dampen a tea towel with water. Set it aside. Divide the dough into 16 small balls and put them in the bowl. Cover the bowl with the tea towel. Take 1 ball and flatten it into a circle on a clean, well-floured work surface. Roll the circle to about 4 inches (10 cm) in diameter using a rolling pin. Cut the dough into circles using a 3-inch (7.5 cm) cookie cutter or the rim of a large glass. Place a ball of filling in the middle of each circle. Working your way around the circle, fold and pleat the dough over the filling, covering it completely, to form a pastry. Place the knishes on a rimmed baking sheet sprayed with nonstick cooking spray and, each time you add one, cover the knishes with a towel to prevent the dough from drying out. Brush the knishes with oil, using your fingertips. Keep making knishes until all the dough is used up. Bake them for 20 to 25 minutes, until they're golden. Serve hot.

building blocks
The primary building block in this recipe is fattiness from the cheddar cheese. An austere red has enough fattiness to match.

flavors
Choose an austere red with earthy tones to match the earthy character of the extra-old cheddar cheese.

late harvest & icewines

PREDOMINANT BUILDING BLOCKS:
Balance of sourness, fruitiness and sweetness.

FLAVORS:
Lychee, melon, grapefruit, pear, apple, mango, banana, raisin, fig, honey, vanilla.

WINES PRODUCED IN THE LATE HARVEST AND ICEWINE STYLE

- Grapes used to produce late harvest wines are left to ripen on the vine into the fall. The wines can sometimes be infected with a beneficial fungus called botrytis (B.A.), giving the resulting wines less fruity and more exotic notes.

- Icewines are made from grapes left to freeze on the vine well into winter. When temperatures reach 17.6°F (-8°C) or lower for three consecutive days, the water inside the grapes is frozen and contains only a small amount of concentrated extract. The grapes are then handpicked and pressed immediately before the sun can thaw some of the water, diluting this concentrate.

- Don't be fooled by imitation or inexpensive icewines. You get what you pay for. Inexpensive ones and fakes are often cloying on the palate and offer no harmonious acidity.

- Late harvest wines and icewines work nicely with all cheeses, fresh fruits and desserts with less sweetness, as well as with hot and spicy cuisine.

The regions at right are stylistically noted for producing late harvest and icewines.

REGIONS

late harvest vidal
Canada (Ontario)

late harvest riesling
Canada (British Columbia, Ontario)

icewines
Gewürztraminer — Canada (Ontario)

Eiswein — Germany

Riesling — Canada (Ontario), Germany

Vidal — Canada (Ontario)

other sweet white dessert wines
Auslese — Germany

Barsac — France

Beerenauslese (B.A.-affected) — Germany

Monbazillac — France

Moscato Passito di Pantelleria — Italy

Muscat de Beaumes-de-Venise (fortified) — France

Sauternes — France

Tokaji Aszú — Hungary

Trockenbeerenauslese (TBA, late harvest and B.A.-affected) — Germany

Vin Santo — Italy

fig tartlets with walnut granola & stilton

Fresh figs were once considered to be sexual stimulants. A man breaking open a fig and eating it in front of his lover was considered a powerful, erotic act.

Serves 4–6 (makes 6 tartlets)

Walnut granola:

3 Tbsp	40 mL	brown sugar
1 Tbsp	15 mL	butter
pinch		cinnamon
pinch		sea salt
6 Tbsp	90 mL	toasted walnut pieces*

Syrup:

½ cup	125 mL	brown sugar
1 Tbsp	15 mL	water
pinch		sea salt
6		fresh figs, stemmed, cut in half, lengthwise
¼ cup	50 mL	butter
¼ cup	50 mL	port

Tartlets:

1		sheet frozen puff pastry (½ package), thawed
3½ oz	105 g	Stilton, crumbled

*Walnuts can be toasted in a dry skillet over medium heat, tossing them frequently, for about 3 minutes.

To make the walnut granola, bring the brown sugar, butter, cinnamon and salt to a boil in a skillet over medium heat, stirring the mixture constantly. Mix in the walnuts. Pour the mixture onto a piece of aluminum foil. Let it cool. When it has cooled, break the mixture into small pieces. Set them aside.

Preheat the oven to 350°F (180°C). To make the syrup, combine the sugar, water and salt in a skillet and cook it on low heat, stirring, until the sugar has melted. Add the figs. Cook the mixture for 5 minutes. Add the butter and port. Remove the mixture from the heat. Remove the figs (reserving the syrup), using a slotted spoon. Let them cool. Place the skillet back on the heat and bring the syrup to a boil. Reduce the heat and simmer the syrup for about 20 minutes, or until it's thick. Keep it warm.

To make the tartlets, roll out the puff pastry on a work surface. Cut out 6 rounds, using a 3-inch (7.5 cm) cookie cutter or the rim of a large glass. Arrange the rounds on a rimmed baking sheet sprayed with nonstick cooking spray. Divide the walnut mixture and place it on the rounds. Place 2 slices of fig on top of the walnut mixture. Bake the tartlets for 30 minutes, or until they're golden. Remove them from the oven. Sprinkle Stilton over the warm tarts. Drizzle syrup over the Stilton. Serve the tartlets warm.

building blocks

The predominant building block is sweetness from the figs and brown sugar. An icewine has enough sweetness to match.

flavors

Choose an icewine with dried fruit flavors to match the flavor of the figs.

pistachio crème brûlée

4		egg yolks
4 Tbsp	50 mL	sugar, divided
½ cup	125 mL	whole milk
½ cup	125 mL	heavy cream
2 tsp	10 mL	pistachio paste*
		sugar (as needed)
6		pistachio nuts
		propane kitchen torch

*If you can't find buy pistachio paste (in a can), which is available at gourmet stores and delicatessens, you can make your own. See the recipe on the facing page.

Preheat the oven to 275°F (120°C). Combine the egg yolks and 2 Tbsp (25 mL) of the sugar in a bowl. Whisk them together until they're well incorporated.

Heat the milk and cream in a small skillet over medium heat. Add the pistachio paste. When the liquid starts to steam, remove the skillet from the heat. Pour some of the liquid into the egg yolks and mix them together quickly. (This heats the yolks slowly, to reduce the chance of curdling.) Start whisking the liquid in the saucepan. Continue to whisk the mixture quickly as you slowly add the egg yolks.

Fill 6 ramekins with the milk and egg mixture. Place the ramekins in a tall-sided baking pan. Fill the pan with simmering water, about halfway up the sides of the ramekins. Bake the custards for 35 to 40 minutes. As they cook in the ramekins, carefully reach into the oven and gently shake one of the ramekins with a pair of tongs toward the end of cooking them, to test whether they're done. The custard's edges should be set but the rest of it should jiggle. Do not overcook the custards; otherwise the mixture will be pasty. Remove the ramekins from the oven. Let them cool. Cover and chill the custards for 2 hours.

When you're ready to serve the crème brûlée, sprinkle the top of each custard with sugar. Heat the sugar until it begins to brown, using a propane kitchen torch; stop when it's golden. Place the remaining pistachio paste in a piping bag and pipe a swirl of paste onto each crème brûlée. Place 1 pistachio nut in the center. Serve each crème brûlée with an espresso spoon.

Pistachio paste:

¼ cup	50 mL	pistachios (skin on)
¼ cup	50 mL	icing sugar
2–4 Tbsp	25–50 mL	water

Grind the pistachios in a food processor or blender. Add the icing sugar and 1 Tbsp (15 mL) of water at a time, until the mixture is a paste that's not liquid, but is thick enough to be shaped into a ball with your hands. Use as directed.

building blocks
The predominant building blocks are fattiness and sweetness from the cream and sugar. An icewine is ideal.

flavors
Choose an icewine with dried fruit flavors to complement the subtle flavor of the pistachios.

silky baked cheesecakes with candied oranges

My good friend Chef Brian Henry made these tarts for his own wedding to replace the traditional wedding cake. I helped him prepare the food and so had the opportunity to taste these tarts as he developed them on the spot. They were so delicious that I asked Chef Brian if I could include the recipe in this book. He willingly agreed, then told me to stop sampling and get back to work! The flavor in this tart is simple, yet delicious. The bright lemon flavor is scrumptious when paired with icewine.

For 4–6 (makes 24 mini cheesecakes)

8 oz	250 g	cream cheese, at room temperature
½ cup	125 mL	granulated sugar
¼ cup	50 mL	liquid honey
1 Tbsp	15 mL	vanilla extract
2 Tbsp	25 mL	all-purpose flour
pinch		cinnamon
¼ cup	50 mL	freshly squeezed lemon juice
		zest of 1 lemon
1		egg
24		unbaked frozen tart shells (2 inches/5 cm in diameter), thawed
		candied oranges (see facing page)

Preheat the oven to 350°F (180°C). Break the cream cheese into chunks in the bowl of an electric mixer or a glass bowl with a hand-held electric mixer. Beat the cream cheese on low to medium speed until it's creamy and smooth. Add the sugar and honey. Resume beating the mixture until it's well mixed. Shut off the mixer and scrape down the sides of the bowl with a spatula. Add the vanilla, flour, cinnamon, lemon juice and lemon zest. Beat them into the cream cheese mixture until they're well incorporated, scraping down the sides of the bowl as needed. Add the egg and beat once more.

Pour the batter into the tart shells, leaving a ⅛-inch (3 mm) space at the top. Bake the tarts for 12 to 14 minutes, or until puffy but not browned on top. Do not let the tops crack. Remove the tarts from the oven and allow them to cool for 1 hour. Decorate them with the candied oranges. Refrigerate the tarts for an additional hour. Serve them chilled.

building blocks
The predominant building block is sweetness from the sugar and honey. An icewine has enough sweetness to match.

flavors
Choose an icewine with citrus tones to marry well with the lemon and candied orange flavors.

Candied oranges:

2		oranges
⅓ cup	75 mL	sugar
⅓ cup	75 mL	water
		sugar for dredging zest strips

Wash the oranges thoroughly. Cut the tops and bottoms off the oranges and score the oranges into quarters, cutting down only into the peel. Do not cut into the flesh. Carefully peel the skins. If the zest strips have any pith (the bitter white layer of the peel) on them, carefully cut or scrape it off with a small knife. Cut the zest strips lengthwise into julienne strips.

Place the zest strips in a small skillet and cover them with cold water. Cook them over medium heat until the water comes to a simmer. Simmer them for 6 minutes. Drain the strips and then return them to the skillet with sugar and water. Bring the mixture to a simmer, then cook it over low heat for 15 minutes, or until the strips turn translucent and the sugar and water begin to thicken.

Remove them from the heat and take the strips from the saucepan, using a fork. Place them on a sheet of wax paper. Separate them and spread out the strips on the wax paper. Allow them to cool slightly. Roll the strips in sugar until they're well coated and allow them to cool completely before storing them in an airtight container. Save the sugar syrup to be used as a sauce or syrup to be drizzled over other desserts.

pumpernickel rounds with caramelized apples, blue cheese & walnuts

This is another recipe I tested on the participants in my Fleming College wine course. It received the thumbs up.

Serves 4–6 (makes 12 rounds)

2		Granny Smith apples
2 Tbsp	25 mL	freshly squeezed lemon juice
¼ cup	50 mL	brown sugar
3 Tbsp	40 mL	butter
4 oz	125 g	blue cheese, crumbled
1 oz	30 g	walnuts, finely chopped
1		stick celery, diced
12		pumpernickel rounds or squares (from a pre-cut loaf of small, round bread)

Peel and core the apples. Slice each apple into 12 wedges. Brush the apple slices with the lemon juice. Sprinkle them with the brown sugar. Melt the butter in a large skillet over medium heat. When the butter starts to bubble, add the apple slices. Cook the apples for 3 minutes, or until they begin to caramelize. Transfer the slices to a dish. Repeat, adding more butter to the pan if needed, until all the slices are caramelized.

Combine the cheese, walnuts and celery in a medium bowl. Place the pumpernickel on a rimmed baking sheet sprayed with nonstick cooking spray. Broil it until it's golden, 1 to 2 minutes. Watch closely, being careful not to burn the bread. Turn each slice and grill the other side. Remove the bread from the oven and let it cool. Spoon the cheese mixture on top of the pumpernickel rounds. Arrange 2 apple slices per round, 12 in total. Serve the pumpernickel rounds warm or at room temperature.

building blocks
The predominant building block is sweetness from the apples. A late harvest white is ideal for this appetizer.

flavors
Choose a late harvest wine with apple and pear flavors to match the flavors in this recipe.

maple hazelnut sour cream ice cream

This is a fabulous rendition of the universal comfort food—ice cream!

Serves 4–6

¼ lb	125 g	hazelnuts
6		egg yolks
1 cup	250 mL	maple syrup
2¼ cups	550 mL	sour cream
1 Tbsp	15 mL	freshly squeezed lemon juice

Preheat the oven to 350°F (180°C). Place the hazelnuts on a rimmed baking sheet sprayed with nonstick cooking spray. Bake them for 10 minutes. Remove them from the oven. Wrap the nuts in a tea towel and rub them to remove their skins. Coarsely chop the nuts in a food processor or blender. Beat the yolks until they're light and fluffy, using an electric mixer. While beating, add the maple syrup in a steady stream until it's fully incorporated. Add the sour cream and lemon juice. Beat the mixture until it's well mixed. Fold in the nuts. Freeze the mixture in an ice cream maker, following the manufacturer's instructions. As soon as it's ready, place each scoop of ice cream in a small ramekin and serve it immediately with an espresso spoon.

building blocks
The predominant building block is sweetness, due to the maple syrup. An icewine has enough sweetness to match.

flavors
Choose an icewine with citrus flavors to offset the rich taste of the maple syrup.

multigrain pancakes topped with asian pear & stilton

Considered a mini-dessert, this dish lets the wine take center stage in the pairing.

Serves 4–6 (makes 12–14 pancakes)

1 cup	250 mL	multigrain flour
2		eggs, lightly beaten
½ cup	125 mL	milk
2 Tbsp	25 mL	finely chopped fresh parsley
2 Tbsp	25 mL	finely chopped fresh sage

Topping:

4 oz	125 g	crumbled Stilton
4 oz	125 g	cream cheese, at room temperature
1		large Asian pear
2 Tbsp	25 mL	finely chopped toasted walnuts*
1		lemon wedge
7		chives, cut in half

*Walnuts can be toasted in a dry skillet over medium heat, tossing them frequently, for about 3 minutes.

Pour the flour into a bowl. Make a well in the center of the flour. Gradually add the eggs and milk, mixing slowly to create a smooth batter. Add more milk, if needed, to thicken the batter. Fold in the fresh herbs.

Spray a large skillet with nonstick cooking spray and heat it over medium heat. Drop 1 Tbsp (15 mL) of the batter into the skillet to make a pancake that's about 2 inches (5 cm) in diameter. Make 4 or 5 at once. Cook the pancakes until the batter begins to bubble at the edges. Turn the pancakes over and cook them until they're golden, about 3 minutes. Let them cool on a rack.

Meanwhile, combine the Stilton and cream cheese in a bowl, mixing them together until smooth. Cut the pear in half. Peel and core one half of the pear. Dice this peeled half into tiny cubes. Fold the cubes of pear into the cheese mixture, along with the walnuts. Set the mixture aside.

Cut the other pear half into thin slices, lengthwise. Cut each slice into 3 triangles. Squeeze lemon juice over the pieces to keep them from browning.

Top each pancake with 1 tsp (5 mL) of the cheese mixture. Arrange the pear triangles on top of the cheese mixture. Place 2 chives, crossing over each other, on top of the pears. Arrange the pancakes on a platter and serve them at room temperature.

building blocks
The predominant building blocks are fattiness from the cheese and fruitiness from the pear. A late harvest wine offers enough body to stand up to, and enough sweetness to harmonize with, the pear.

flavors
Choose a late harvest wine with apple and pear flavors to enhance the delicate taste of the Asian pear.

orgasmic appetizers to pair with port & port-style wines

Port & port-style wines

PREDOMINANT BUILDING BLOCKS:

Dry versions have fruitiness and sourness and umami.

Sweet versions have fruitiness with balanced sourness, some bitterness and umami.

FLAVORS:

Nutty, toasty, smoky-spicy, caramelized, woody, chocolatey, hazelnut, raisin, plum and prune.

PORT AND WINES PRODUCED IN THE PORT STYLE

- Port is the quintessential after-dinner drink. However, with a slice of lemon, served over ice, it's also a fabulous summer refresher.

- This style of wine ranges in sweetness and works well with desserts. Due to its sugar levels and high alcohol content, port is fatty and therefore works with fatty savory dishes, as well.

- Best savory food matches include duck, fois gras and game meats, especially when these items are cooked with or accompanied by port-infused sauces.

- Wines produced in this style, both white and red, are fortified with a spirit, such as grape brandy.

- Because of the added alcohol and aging of ports and some port-style wines, they possess synergistic umami.

- Port is loosely divided into two categories: wood-aged and bottle-aged.

- Wood-aged ports are matured in oak and ready to drink when bottled. They include white port, ruby port (*tinto aloirado*) and tawny port (*aloirado*).

- Ruby is young and fruity and harmonizes with goat cheeses.

- White port complements crumbly cheeses, fruit-based desserts and white chocolate.

- Tawny port ranges in age from 3 to 5 years and offers nutty character. Aged versions can be as old as 50 years. This style works with hard sheep's milk cheeses, as well as apple pie, crème brûlée, fruitcake and biscotti. Dark chocolate is also a fabulous partner.

- Bottle-aged ports are left to mature in the bottle. They include vintage port, single Quinta vintage port, port wine with the date of harvest, crusted or vintage-character port and late-bottled vintage port (LBV). Only vintage ports (bottle aged) require decanting as they throw sediment.

- Vintage port works with a variety of blue cheeses and hazelnut chocolate torte.

The regions below are stylistically noted for producing port and port-style wines.

REGIONS

port — *Portugal*

Crusted

LBV

Ruby

Single Quinta

Tawny

10-year-old tawny

20-, 30- and 40-year-old tawny

Vintage

White

others

Mavrodaphne of Patras — Greece

Muscadel — South Africa

Port-style — Australia, Canada (British Columbia, Ontario), New Zealand, United States (California)

country-style duck pâté toasts

This is a country-style rendition of that rich and expensive delicacy, foie gras pâté. The addition of port to this recipe helps to add some umami, for depth of flavor.

Serves 4–6
(makes 16 toasts)

3 oz	90 g	duck fat
1		shallot, diced
3 oz	90 g	duck liver, chopped
¼ tsp	1 mL	herbes de Provence
2		cloves garlic, minced
		sea salt to taste
		freshly ground black pepper to taste
1 tsp	5 mL	white port
16		slices toasted baguette

Heat the duck fat in a skillet over medium heat. Add the shallot and sauté it in the fat. Add the duck liver, the herbes de Provence and the garlic. Cook the mixture for 2 minutes, stirring it occasionally. Season it with salt and pepper. Add the duck fat mixture to a food processor or blender. Add the port. Blend the mixture until it's liquefied. Transfer it to a serving bowl. Let it cool. Cover it and refrigerate it for at least 2 hours. Serve the pâté at room temperature with slices of toasted baguette.

building blocks
The predominant building block is fattiness from the duck fat and liver. A white port has enough fattiness and weight to match.

flavors
Choose a white port with some sweetness to offset the gamy flavor of the duck.

umami cheese ball

Make this recipe the night before your event to allow the flavors to meld. With the three cheese varieties and bacon, this cheese ball is loaded with umami, so it works nicely with any high-alcohol or fortified wine such as port.

Serves 4–6

8 oz	250 g	cream cheese, at room temperature
½ cup	125 mL	milk
2 cups	500 mL	shredded extra-old cheddar cheese
2 cups	500 mL	shredded Colby
¼ cup	50 mL	crumbled roquefort
12		slices cooked bacon, crumbled
¾ cup	175 mL	chopped walnuts
¼ cup	50 mL	finely chopped red onion
2 oz	60 g	diced pimento, drained
		sea salt to taste
		freshly ground black pepper to taste
¼ cup	50 mL	finely chopped fresh parsley
1 Tbsp	15 mL	poppy seeds
		toasted baguette slices

Cream the cream cheese and milk in a bowl, using a handheld electric mixer or an upright mixer. Add the cheddar cheese, Colby and roquefort. Fold in half the bacon, half the nuts, half the onion and half the pimento. Season the mixture with salt and pepper. Divide the mixture in half and shape each half into a ball. Wrap the cheese balls tightly in plastic wrap and refrigerate them for about 2 hours. Combine the remaining bacon, nuts, onion and pimento in a bowl. Add the parsley and poppy seeds. Remove the cheese balls from the plastic wrap. Roll the balls in the bacon and poppy seed mixture, coating them completely. Wrap the coated balls in new plastic wrap and refrigerate them overnight. Serve at room temperature with toasted baguette.

building blocks
The predominant building blocks are fattiness and saltiness, due to the cheeses and bacon. Tawny port, due to its high alcohol content, has enough fattiness to match.

flavors
Choose a tawny port with a nutty flavor to enhance the flavor of the walnuts.

tea-infused dark chocolate truffles

Chocolate is believed to contain a substance called fenyletylamin, a natural version of amphetamine. It causes the sensation of happiness and so could be considered an aphrodisiac.

Serves 4–6 (makes 24 truffles)

⅔ cup	150 mL	heavy cream
2 Tbsp	25 mL	unsalted butter, at room temperature
1		black tea tea bag
6 oz	175 g	bittersweet chocolate (86 percent cocoa or higher), in small pieces
1 cup	250 mL	unsweetened cocoa powder

Combine the cream and butter in a skillet set over high heat. Bring it to a high simmer, almost a boil. Reduce the heat to low. Add the tea bag. Let it steep for 5 minutes, or until the cream tastes of tea. Remove the tea bag and discard it. Add the chocolate to the cream, stirring constantly until it's melted. Transfer the mixture to a glass bowl. Cover it and refrigerate it for about 2 hours, until it's firm but not hard.

Pour ½ cup (125 mL) of the cocoa powder into a bowl. Dust your hands with the cocoa powder. Put 1 tsp (5 mL) of the chocolate mixture in the palm of your hand. Roll it into a ball and then roll the ball in cocoa powder, coating it lightly. Set the truffle on a serving plate. Repeat, making about 24 truffles. Cover the plate with plastic wrap and refrigerate it until it's ready to serve. (You may have enough truffle mixture left over to use for another recipe, depending on the size of your truffles.) Serve the truffles at room temperature.

building blocks
The predominant building blocks are sweetness and bitterness from the dark chocolate and tea. A tawny port with sweetness and a finish of bitterness is a good match.

flavors
Choose a tawny port with nutty flavors to harmonize with the flavor of the dark chocolate.

buckwheat blini with gorgonzola

Buckwheat blini are rich, yeasty pancakes with enough weight and flavor to match a port wine. You can alter the toppings, using goat cheese or cheddar cheese, as well.

*Serves 4–6
(makes 60 blini)*

1½ cups	375 mL	milk
½ oz	15 g	fresh yeast
¼ lb	125 g	buckwheat flour
¼ lb	125 g	all-purpose flour
¼ tsp	1 mL	salt
½ tsp	2 mL	ground caraway seeds
½ tsp	2 mL	ground sesame seeds
2 tsp	10 mL	honey
1 tsp	5 mL	unsalted butter
1		egg, separated

Gorgonzola topping:

8 oz	250 g	Gorgonzola
¼ cup	50 mL	toasted sesame seeds*

*To toast the sesame seeds, place them in a dry skillet over medium heat, tossing them until they're toasted.

Mix 2 Tbsp (25 mL) of the milk with the yeast in a cup. Let the mixture stand for 10 to 15 minutes, allowing the yeast to activate. Sift the flours and salt into a bowl. Add the caraway and sesame seeds. Make a well in the flour mixture. Heat the milk with the honey and butter in a small skillet over low heat. Remove it from the heat. Stir the yeast mixture into the warm milk. Blend in the egg yolk. Pour the liquid mixture into the well in the flour mixture. Blend them together, using a wooden spoon. Beat the dough by hand for 2 minutes. Let it stand for 1 hour, until the dough has risen and is bubbly. (The dough should drop easily from a teaspoon. If it's too thick, add a little warm water.)

Spray a large skillet with nonstick cooking spray and set it on medium heat. Drop 1 tsp (5 mL) of batter at a time into the skillet. Flatten each blini with the back of a spatula so the disks are about 2 inches (5 cm) in diameter. Cook the blini until bubbles form on top. Flip them over and cook them for another minute. Place the blini on a rimmed baking sheet sprayed with nonstick cooking spray, covered with a cloth. Place them in the oven at its lowest temperature.

To make the topping, cream the Gorgonzola in a bowl. Place ½ tsp (2 mL) of cheese on each warm blini. Sprinkle the blini with sesame seeds and serve them warm.

building blocks
The predominant building blocks are fattiness and saltiness in the blue cheese. A ruby port has enough fattiness to match.

flavors
Choose a ruby port with fruity character to harmonize with the flavor of the Gorgonzola.

Seasonings

Please note that these dry rubs are not the same as Cajun Quickie, Sweet Jerk and Tickle My Ribs, which are specially formulated to complement specific styles of wine. They are available exclusively from Orgasmic Culinary Creations. Turn to the last page for ordering information.

creole seasoning

Makes about 1⅓ cups (325 mL)

¾ cup	175 mL	salt
¼ cup	50 mL	ground cayenne pepper
2 Tbsp	25 mL	white pepper
2 Tbsp	25 mL	ground black pepper
2 Tbsp	25 mL	paprika
2 Tbsp	25 mL	onion powder
2 Tbsp	25 mL	garlic powder

Place all the ingredients in a food processor or blender. Mix until well blended. Store the rub in an airtight container at room temperature.

jamaican seasoning

*Makes about
½ cup (125 mL)*

2 Tbsp	25 mL	dried, minced onion
2 tsp	10 mL	dried thyme
2 tsp	10 mL	ground allspice
2 tsp	10 mL	ground black pepper
2 tsp	10 mL	cinnamon
½ tsp	2 mL	cayenne pepper
½ tsp	2 mL	salt

Place all the ingredients in a food processor or blender. Mix until well blended. Store the rub in an airtight container at room temperature.

all-purpose dry rub

Makes 2 cups (500 mL)

1½ cups	375 mL	brown sugar
⅓ cup	75 mL	seasoned salt
2 Tbsp	15 mL	paprika
1 tsp	5 mL	cayenne pepper
1 tsp	5 mL	cumin
1 tsp	5 mL	ground coriander
1 tsp	5 mL	crushed dried rosemary
1 tsp	5 mL	curry powder
1 tsp	5 mL	dried mustard
1 tsp	5 mL	ground allspice
1 tsp	5 mL	ground ginger
1 tsp	5 mL	ground mace
1 tsp	5 mL	white pepper

Place all the ingredients in a food processor or blender. Mix until well blended. Store the rub in an airtight container at room temperature.

Page numbers in bold indicate tables, illustrations or photographs.

Acknowledgments

I want to thank the experts who have contributed to this book or whose books have inspired me. Thank you for your ingenuity, generosity and expertise.

Sonoe Sugawara, PR & Marketing Manager, Umami Information Center

David and Anna Kasabian, authors of *The Fifth Taste: Cooking with Umami*

Hervé This, author of *Molecular Gastronomy: Exploring the Science of Flavor*

Gray Kunz and Peter Kaminsky, authors of *The Elements of Taste*

Linda Bartoshuk, PhD Research Scientist, Otolaryngology, Yale University School of Medicine

A special thank you to all the chefs, cooks and wine lovers who generously contributed their orgasmic recipes to this book.

Chef David Franklin
Chef Brian Henry
Garry and Eleanor Humphries
Chef Ritchie Kukle
Sharon Aubie
Michael Hunter, Stargazers on the Thames, Pain Court, Ontario
Chef Mike Szabo
Laura Northey
Sadie Darby
Susan Lunn
Jay Bulgin, my brother
Chef Michael Knowlson, Sequoia Grill, Vancouver
Michelle Ramsay

Chef Andy Chong, Vancouver Golf Club
Chef Jeff Crump, Ancaster Old Mill Restaurant in Ancaster
Grant Zwarych
Chef Anne Kaukonen, Appetizers and More
Chef Steve Benns, Fleming College
Ron Walker, Fleming College
Cathy Ruggieri-Davidson, LCBO Consultant
Lisa Alguire, Colio Wines
Montana's Restaurant
Mom and Dad

Lastly, thank you to my recipe-testing team,
who so graciously provided feedback and suggestions.

Les and Brenda Bulgin
Debbie Crossen
Brenda Lachance
Michelle Leduc
Sharon Aubie
Laura Northey
Jay Bulgin
Ron Walker
Lori Gill
Denise Payne
Michael Gravelle and Sue Pulfer
Carol-Ann Julson

make your guests moan with ecstasy

Orgasmic Culinary Creations produces a line of artisan dry rubs and food products for the wine lover. The Orgasmic dry rubs are handmade and individually created, and their seasonings and measurements have been carefully selected to harmonize with certain wine styles. When served with specific wines, the foods you season with these rubs will have you and your guests moaning in ecstasy.

To order Orgasmic Culinary Creation products, go to: www.orgasmicculinarycreations.com

cajun quickie: a blackening dry rub for vegetables, fish, seafood, pork and beef

sweet jerk: a jerk heat-and-spice dry rub for vegetables, fish, seafood, chicken and pork

tickle my ribs: a caramelizing dry rub for pork and beef ribs

The Creation of Orgasmic Culinary Creations

Shari Darling has been conducting wine and food pairing workshops for organizations and corporations across Canada and the US for more than 15 years. She created a Sweet Jerk dry rub to use in her educational workshops so participants could experience, firsthand, how hot and spicy seasonings complement certain wines.

She realized that Sweet Jerk had taken on a life of its own. It appealed to wine lovers, and she realized it was her job to ensure that wine lovers could buy it. When she shared the news that Sweet Jerk was coming to market, her clients purchased more than a thousand bags. She has been busy fulfilling orders ever since.

Today, Sweet Jerk, Cajun Quickie, Tickle My Ribs, French Kiss, Salt Lover's Rib Rub and other artisan products for the wine lover are available on her website as well as at gourmet retail and wine shops across Canada.

Each Orgasmic dry rub contains three pimento berries. One berry represents the wine, the second berry represents the food and the third berry represents the harmony between them.